They Spoke With God

They Spoke With God

Saints of Tamizhaham

Sethu Ramaswamy

D.K. Printworld (P) Ltd.
New Delhi

Cataloging in Publication Data — DK

[Courtesy: D.K. Agencies (P) Ltd. <docinfo@dkagencies.com>]

Ramaswamy, Sethu, 1924-
They spoke with god : saints of Tamizhaham / Sethu
Ramaswamy.
p. cm.
ISBN 13: 9788124605363
ISBN 10: 812460536X

1. Śaivites — India — Tamil Nadu — Biography. 2. Hindu saints, Tamil — Biography. 3. Śaivism — India — Tamil Nadu — History. I. Title.

DDC 294.551309225482 22

First published in India, 2009

ISBN 13: 978-81-246-0536-3 (PB) ISBN 10: 81-246-0536-X

Published and printed by:
D.K. Printworld (P) Ltd.
Regd. office : *'Srikunj,'* F-52, Bali Nagar
Ramesh Nagar Metro Station
New Delhi – 110 015
Phones : (011) 2545 3975; 2546 6019; *Fax* : (011) 2546 5926
E-mail: dkprintworld@vsnl.net
Web: www.dkprintworld.com

Dedicated in the memory of

My mother
K. Anandammal

Storyteller *par excellence*

Foreword

THE lives of saints have held a lasting fascination for Indians then and now. Given the fact that our society has a strong religious substratum, saints have emerged in our midst as votaries of peace, transcendence and mysticism, commanding much love and respect among the people.

This monograph: *They Spoke With God: Saints of Tamizhaham* by Sethu Ramaswamy, describes the life and times of some prominent saints of Tamizhaham or Tamil Nadu. The saints chosen here were by and large exponents of the Shaivaite path of devotion. The author hopes to follow it up by detailing the lives and teachings of Vaishnavaite saints. Beginning with the lives of Nayanar saints like Somasimarar Nayanar, Nandanar, Karaikkal Ammaiyar, Pusalur Nayanar and Kannappa Nayanar, the narration moves on to the medieval *bhakti* saints. The concluding part deals with the ecstatic lives of late nineteenth- and twentieth-century saints like Seshadhri Swamigal, Kuzhandaiyananda, Senthamangalam Swayam Prakasa Swamigal and the saint-composer Andavan Pichchai Amma, a woman saint of our own times.

The lives of these saints have been simply told without making their message complex. Every saint was different, the path they trod was different and yet all these amazing men and women had one thing in common — their saintliness. Some were articulate like Andavan Pichchai and some like Sadasiva Brahmendra did not speak at all. Some lived all their lives in one place in silent meditation, and some like Seshadhri Swami acted in a spirit of divine madness. One woman saint has described this state of divine intoxication as "spiritual hysteria." Despite the range of differences in behavioural patterns, these saints shared the quality of ecstasy of an unending celebration of "the life divine." The purpose of narrating the lives of these saints is to capture this celebratory quality of their lives which is seen in their poems and musical compositions.

The present collection is specially targeted at young readers from the age of eight to eighteen. It is aimed at introducing the younger generation to our rich spiritual and cultural legacy. It is also intended for a wider readership comprising both young and old — Indian and Western — with either intellectual curiosity or inclination for the spiritual path.

Some of these stories are being introduced to an English-speaking audience for the first time — for instance the lives of Cendamangalam Swamigal and Andavan Pichchai Amma. Their incredible life stories and spiritual journeys may turn out to be eye-openers for even those well versed in our spiritual tradition. It is noteworthy that the accounts of the lives of these saints are based on the first-hand experience of Sethu Ramaswamy as well as her mother Anandammal Ramaswamy. Therefore, unlike the narration of the lives of other saints, the life of Andavan Pichchai is a personalised and subjective narrative by the author.

It is hoped that these deeply inspiring and illuminating lives will make a difference in the lives of those who read about them.

Vijaya Ramaswamy

Acknowledgements

The stories of the Saints in Part II and some featuring in Part III are partially based on the Late Srimati Gomathi Rajangam's book *Sidhar Varalaru* in Tamil. To my family friend, and a great Sanskrit scholar, I am indebted.

The pictures of Avudai Akkal and her Guru Ayyaval are taken from the Shencottah Sri Avudai Akkal Padal Thirattu, published by Sri Gnanananda Niketan, Thapovan. The pictures of saints belonging to the Pundukkottai Adhishtanam, published by Krishnasami Chettiar were provided to me by Mr. G.V. Subramaniam and my son-in-law N.S. Mani. To them my thanks. The pictures of Svami Kuzhandaiyananda and Sri Seshadri Svamigal were accessed from the website.

Many thanks to my daughter Vijaya who has always undertaken the task of correcting, typing and making my writings printworthy. She chose my publisher D.K. Printworld (P) Ltd. who graciously accepted my manuscript and has shown keenness in bringing it out soon. As an author of 85, I wish them to rise to greater heights in the Publishing Industry.

My grateful thanks to my son-in-law Krish for meticulously correcting the proofs, and to my eight year old grandson Ram will go the first copy of this book for his pestering me with the question "when is your book coming patti"?

Sethu Ramaswamy

Contents

Part III
Saints of Modern Period

List of Illustrations

Introduction to the Periya Puranam

Periya Puranam is commonly regarded as the most important collection of the lives of Shaivaite saints believed to have been written by Chekkizhar. The text in terms of its historical location has been placed anywhere between the eighth and the twelfth centuries although now most scholars hold that the latter date is more probable. A popular folklore foregrounds the writing of this text. The folk tradition is as follows:

Anapayan Chola Raja was a devotee of Lord Shiva, but he also read and admired the life of a Jain King Jeevaraj, in a book titled *Chintamani*. Devout Shaivaites questioned the king about his admiration for a mere king, when the stories of the Shaivaite saints were so edifying and purifying. They compared the king's taste for *Chintamani*, to the taste of the juice of the *neem*, and the taste of the lives of the Shaivaite saints to the sweetness of sugar cane juice.

The king then asked them, "where is such a book? Who has written it? Who has read it? Who has heard about it? And who has spoken about it? Please let me know, so that I can also benefit by reading about the lives of the Shaivaite saints." The poet Chekhizhar who was present then explained to the king, how Lord Shiva in Tiruvaroor had commanded his dearest friend and devotee Sundaramoorthy to sing the praise of the Lord as the humblest servant of His devotees. The first line begins as directed by the Lord *tillaivazh anthanar tham adiyarkum adiyen*, meaning "I am the servant of the servants of the brahmins of Tillai."

The eleven verses that Sundaramoorthy sang contain the stories of all the 63 Shaivaite Saints. This was in turn re-written by Tirunarayoor Nambyandan Nambi. Hearing the praise of these wondrous stories the king Anapayan commanded the poet Sekhizhar to write in prose the lives of the 63 Shaivaite saints. Sekhizhar then visited Chidambaram and prayed to Lord Nataraja to guide him in this project. Suddenly all who were present there heard a divine voice from the *sanctum sanctorum* saying "begin with the words — *ulakellam unarnthorkariyavar*" meaning "He who cannot be known even by the wisest."

Anapayan Chola Maharaja heard of this miracle and immediately went to Chidambaram and fell at the feet of Sekhizhar and requested him to narrate the *Periya Puranam* stories of the lives of the 63 Shaivaite saints to him and to all the devotees of Shiva. It was the month of Chithirai — the first month of the Tamil year.

Lord Nataraja's birth star was Tiruvathirai, and the boy-saint Tirugnana Sambandhar — with the same birth star Tiruvathirai — was breastfed by the divine mother Parvati on Tiruvadirai day in the month of Chithirai. Therefore Sekhizhar proposed to begin the narration of the *Periya Puranam* on Tiruvathirai day and end it the next year in the month of Chithirai on the day when the star Tiruvadhirai would be in the ascendant.

I will attempt in the following pages a free rendering of some of the stories from the Tamil *Periya Puranam*.

Part I

Stories from the Periya Puranam

Treasure House of Shaivaite Hagiographies

1

Somasi Marar Nayanar

On the edges of the city of Tiruvaroor there lived a poor brahmin (who was later to be known as Somasi Marar Nayanar); he was a great devotee of Lord Shiva. His days were spent in gathering flowers and sacred leaves for the worship of Shiva. He lived in a small hut on a patch of land which he owned, in which he grew flowers and leafy greens for his food.

His one great ambition and desire was to perform the most sacred and difficult *Soma-Yaga*, and to invoke Lord Shiva himself to appear in person to accept the *havir bhagam*, an offering of cooked rice with clarified butter — a special offering to Shiva at the conclusion of the *Yaga*. He wanted nothing else in life — neither wealth nor family.

With this sole purpose in his heart and mind he prayed and prayed everyday that this wish of his be fulfilled. As days passed by he despaired of ever being able to save enough money to conduct the *Soma-Yaga*, and most important, how could he get Shiva to come in person to accept the *havir bhagam*?

People in the village observed the pious brahmin. One day a few of the villagers came to the brahmin's hut on a friendly visit. They found him gathering flowers for his daily worship. While talking to him they came to know about his cherished dream of performing the *Soma-Yaga* and invoking Lord Shiva himself to accept the *havir bhagam*. The usual practice was to invoke Lord Shiva and give the offering to a brahmin representing Shiva. But this brahmin wanted Shiva himself to accept the *havir bhagam*!

The villagers who had come to visit the brahmin were very wise men. They told him that, if that was his desire, he should approach Sri Sundaramoorthy the great devotee and friend of Tiruvaroor deity Shiva. They said that they had heard that Sundarar meets Shiva in the temple daily and they converse. Lord Shiva would do anything for his friend Sundarar. After giving this valuable advice the villagers left.

The poor brahmin was overjoyed, but immediately he fell into despondency. How was he a poor brahmin to get near the great Sundarar who lived like a prince with his two wives in a palace, let alone talk to him! The brahmin thought and thought and at last decided on a plan.

Next day early in the morning he picked a bunch of leaves from the *Thoothuvalangai* plant. He had grown these berries in the small patch of land he had. When he had a good bunch of the leaves of this plant which was prepared like spinach, he wrapped them up in a plantain leaf and started for the temple town of Tiruvaroor which was across the river.

The brahmin reached the palace of Sundarar within an hour. He went to the rear side and entered the kitchen. He gave the bunch of greens to the head cook and told him how to prepare it, with the request that it should be served to his master everyday. He told the cook he would bring the greens everyday. From that day onwards Sri Sundaramoorthy was served *Thoothuvalangai keerai* (greens) on his plantain leaf in addition to the various other delicacies included in his lunch.

Thus more than a month passed by and still the brahmin did not have an opportunity of meeting the great Sundarar. His prayers to Lord Shiva became more intense.

Suddenly one night it started raining. It not only rained, but there was a heavy downpour, and in the morning the usually low level water in the river started swelling due to flooding. That morning the brahmin could not wade across the river to reach the temple town of Tiruvaroor to give the greens to the cook to prepare it for his master's lunch. That afternoon when Sundaramoorthy sat down for lunch he found one item missing. He had become quite fond of the *Thoothuvalangai keerai*. He called the cook and asked why it was not served. The cook then told him about the poor brahmin from across the river who daily brought the greens from his garden but could not come today because the river was in spate. Sundarar expressed a wish to see the brahmin and ordered that he should be brought to him when he came the next time.

The rains stopped and the brahmin took his bunch of greens to Sundaramoorthy's palace kitchen. As soon as he came the cook asked him to stay and not go away as the master wanted to meet him. He narrated what happened when the greens were not served for the master's lunch.

The brahmin was overjoyed at the prospect of meeting the great Sundarar, but waited with trepidation at meeting the great man. He knew this was the opportunity he was waiting for and prayed to Lord Shiva for courage to speak out his request.

The cook informed his master that the brahmin who brought the *Thoothuvalangai keerai* was here. Sundarar immediately ordered another leaf to be laid for the brahmin and invited him to have lunch with him.

The poor brahmin was so overwhelmed, and was shrinking with humility. He prostrated before Sundarar who embraced him and said that he was honoured to have him as a guest.

After lunch Sundarar asked the brahmin "now, tell me what can I do for you?" The brahmin in all humility said "Sir, I have heard that you are a bosom friend of Lord Shiva of Tiruvaroor and converse with him daily in the temple. My appeal to you is to make a request on my behalf to your friend Lord Shiva to come in person and accept the offering of *havir bhagam* when I perform the *Soma-Yaga*."

Sundaramoorthy thought for a while and said "Do not think that because I converse with the Lord daily, I can order Him to do whatever I want. He is God and I am His humble devotee. But this much I will do for you, I will let Him know your wish. If he so pleases He may accede to your request. But how He will come, whether He will come at all, I cannot guarantee you. I cannot promise you anything."

The brahmin went away happy. He made all arrangements for the *Soma-Yaga* to be performed for which he had been saving money for years. He sold his land and everything that he had. He invited learned Pundits who were well-versed in conducting the *yaga*.

The great day came. Very early in the morning the *yaga* commenced. For three days the sacred fire was kept ablaze with ghee, incense and huge bundles of twigs called *samit* from the Bo tree.

On the final day and the final hour the time for invoking Lord Shiva and offering Him the *havir bhagam* came — the learned brahmins raised their voices in chanting the *mantra*s to a high and loud pitch — the atmosphere was electrifying — when suddenly like a great gust of wind, a motley crowd from the *Paraicheri* (Dalit or Pariah settlement) descended on the sacred place where the *yaga* was being performed.

The leader of the crowd was a dirty unkempt man with long matted hair, spit rolling from the corner of his mouth, eyes red and four dirty pariah dogs — two hanging on each shoulder. A woman walked beside him, apparently his wife; she was equally unkempt, chewing something in her mouth, with uncombed, unwashed long hair. The other were all unsavoury looking, filthy men, women and children marching behind their leader laughing loudly and singing.

The brahmins had just concluded the *mantra*s for the offering of *havir bhagam* to Shiva. On seeing this dirty Pariah crowd they fled away shouting *abhacharam, abhacharam* — and *brashtam* — meaning "polluted and defiled!"

The brahmin who had been waiting for this moment all his life ecstatically got up and offering the *havir bhagam* to the Pariah leader fell at his feet and held both the feet of the leader with his hands and his head touching the feet chanted "Shiva, Shiva, my Lord, I am blessed."

The people of the town who had come in large numbers to witness the conclusion of this great *yaga* were surprised and shocked at this behaviour of the brahmin — as for the learned *pundit*s they were nowhere to be seen.

The Pariah leader lifted up the brahmin and partaking of the *havir bhagam*, he gave his wife a portion — and lo! The brahmin saw before him the dazzling vision of Lord Parameshwara and Parvati. The dirty motley crowd turned out to be Shiva's heavenly servants. The four dogs were the Vedas. Sundaramoorthy who was with the poor brahmin throughout the *yaga* had a special smile and grateful thanks for his divine friend.

Needless to say the poor brahmin was no longer "poor," he was filled with joy and was in an ecstasy having received the vision and grace of Shiva and Parvati. The whole of Tiruvaroor was blessed with the darshan of Lord Shiva except the learned *pundit*s who had run away.

Sundaramoorthy — one of the Nayanars — himself has written the life of the poor pious brahmin and called him Somasi Marar Nayanar.

The life of Somasi Marar Nayanar is proof that God is in everyone and everything and can come before us in any form. If the saint had turned away from the unkempt crowd he would not have had the blessed vision of his beloved Shiva. His biography inspires us to be in a state of preparedness to meet with God whether he assumes a divine form or a most lowly one.

2

Kannappa Nayanar

NAGAN was the king of a hunter tribe. His queen's name was Thathai. He ruled the fertile land of Pottapi and lived in a hamlet called Udupoor.

Long years after marriage they still had no child. They were very unhappy about it, and decided to pray to Muruga, Lord of Kurunji. Muruga's emblems were the cock and his *vahanam*, the peacock, so they sent many cocks and peacocks to the temple. They prayed intensely to Muruga to bless them with a child.

Their prayers were answered and with Lord Muruga's blessings, Thathai conceived. A son was born, and Nagan and his tribesmen were very happy. Nagan took the child in his arms and found him very heavy so he called him Thinnan, a word meaning plump and healthy.

The child Thinnan grew up to be a fine young man, very well-versed in the art of archery. The bow and arrow and the sword were the weapons of the hunter tribe to hunt animals for their food.

As Nagan was getting old and could not go on these hunting expeditions, he appointed his son Thinnan as his successor. Thinnan took command of the hunters and went out with them for hunting.

One day, a big fat pig caught in a net laid by the hunters, broke loose and escaped. It ran for its life as fast as its legs could go. Thinnan saw the pig escape and went after it. Two of his men followed him. Thinnan had to run a long way before he finally caught up with the pig and slashed it into two with his sword. His two men Nanan and Kadan praised him for killing the pig after such a hot chase. They said the running had made them hungry and they wanted to roast the pig at once to appease their hunger and drink water to wash the meat down. But Thinnan wanted to roast the pig only where water was available. Nanan pointed out a cluster of teak trees and told Thinnan that there was a mountain beyond those trees, and the Ponmukali river flowed there. Thinnan asked them to carry the pig there. As they were walking towards the river, Thinnan saw the mountain Tirukkalahasti and immediately expressed a desire that he wanted to go up the mountain. Nanan said it was a good idea as Kudumi Thevar (Shiva with his knot of hair on his head) is on top of the mountain and they could worship Him. As he approached the mountain Kalahasti, Thinnan felt his heavy body becoming lighter. He was excited at this change in him and wondered what else was in store for him!

They reached the river Ponmukali and deposited the pig under the shade of a tree. Thinnan ordered Kadan to light a fire and keep it ready for roasting the pig, while he and Nanan climbed the mountain to worship the deity. Nanan and Thinnan crossed the river and came to mount Tirukkalahasti. They climbed the mountain and reached the place where the *Shivalinga* was. The moment Thinnan set eyes on the sacred *Shivalinga* there was a sudden change in him, it was as if a piece of iron had magically turned into gold. He was not the same Thinnan the hunter, he was one with Shiva. Like a mother who has been separated from her long-lost child and suddenly finds him, he embraced the *linga*, he kissed Him and fondled Him like a child. For a long time he stood speechless, his whole body in an ecstasy, tears streaming from his eyes. Like a candle melting in the sun's heat his heart melted with love for the Lord.

He cried out "what a wonder it is that I have found you O Lord!" Immediately he fell into a mood of concern for the Lord who was alone, among wild beasts roaming the forest. His heart was overcome with sadness at the plight of the Lord, who was at the mercy of dangerous wild beasts. In his agitation his bow and arrows slipped to the ground. He took control of himself and looked closely at Shiva and was surprised to see that someone had poured water on Him and placed fresh flowers and leaves on his head. "Who could have done this?," he wondered aloud. Nanan who was near him said "a long time ago I used to come here with your father when we went hunting and we saw a brahmin pouring water on the deity's head and placing flowers and leaves, offering food and muttering something before the deity. Perhaps it is the same person who has come here today."

When he heard this Thinnan understood that this was the way to worship and please Shiva and he decided to do the same. He wanted to offer the meat of the pig as food for the Lord, but how could he bear to be separated from his beloved even for a minute? At the same time if he did not go and bring the meat how could he feed Him? Determined to go, he went some distances and turning saw Shiva and came running back and held him tightly to his chest. Again he forced himself to go and yet again like a cow reluctant to leave her baby calf he came back. At last he steeled himself, took up his bow and arrows, bowed his head before the Lord and left. He crossed the river and reached the bank where Kadan was waiting with a roaring fire. He greeted Thinnan and wanted to know the reason for the delay in their return. Nanan was quick to answer, "oh, he was so smitten by the *Shivalinga*, that he clung to Him. Even now he has come only to take back the pig's meat for the Lord's food. He has given up his leadership of his tribe — he now belongs to that Svami." Kadan was alarmed "O, Thinnan, what have you done! Why have you gone mad over this God?," he cried.

Thinnan hardly heeded them as he was busy roasting the pig, prodding the fleshy tender portions with his arrow, breaking the pieces, piercing them through with his arrow and turning the arrow over the fire in order to roast them. When the meat was cooked he chewed the pieces and set aside the tender bits and spat out the rest. Thus he ensured that only the tender pieces would be given to the Lord.

Seeing this the fears of Nanan and Kadan were confirmed about Thinnan's madness in keeping aside all the meat when they were all hungry and did not have the chance to eat any portion of it. They decided he was possessed by the God and wanted to inform his father Nagan and his mother about his madness and come back with a strong contingent of hunters to tackle this problem.

Thinnan was quite oblivious to all that was happening and to the departure of Nanan and Kadan. He packed the meat in the bark of the teak tree, filled his mouth with water for pouring on the head of Shiva, and plucked some flowers and stuck them in his hair. He then climbed the mountain and came to the place where the *Shivalinga* was. He spat out the water from his mouth on Shiva's head, plucked out the flowers from his head and put them on the *linga* and sat down to feed Shiva. He then took out the meat and coaxed Shiva to partake of it telling Him how he had chewed and tasted and brought the tender pieces for Him. As he offered each piece he praised the sweet taste of the meat and offered it to him with great love, cajoling Him to have a little more.

The sun set and darkness enveloped the forest. Thinnan in order to protect the Lord from the wild beasts roaming the forest, took up his stand near the *Shivalinga* and without closing his eyes even for a second spent the whole night in vigil.

The next day Thinnan went to hunt for food to serve this Lord. Shivakocharyar was a saint with qualities of humility, knowledge and devotion to Shiva, all combined to make him a truly great saint. Sorrow or happiness left him unaffected. He had a serene and captivating manner which charmed all those who met him. This great Shivakocharyar would daily climb the mountain Kalahasti and worship Lord Shiva according to the true Shaiva Agama ritual at the dawn of the day. He would bring water from the river Ponmukali and perform *abhishekam*, chanting the *Rudram-Chamakam*. He would perform worship or *archana* with the sacred vilva leaves and other flowers, and offer prasad to the deity.

That day when he came, he found the place strewn with meat pieces and bones. He was shocked and shivered with fear and ran to the *Shivalinga* and cried aloud "O Lord, who has done this? Only these hunters could have done this sacrilege. How could you permit it my Lord" he wailed. He then set about cleaning the place and washing it with water. He again went to the river Ponmukali and had bath for a second time and came back with water. He first sprinkled water all over the place chanting a *mantra* to purify it. He then performed the ritual of *abhisheka* for Shiva chanting the *Rudram-Chamakam* He performed *archana* with the flowers and sacred leaves he had brought. He offered the *prasada* he had brought and lifting both hands high on to his head with emotion chanted the *Samaveda* hymns. He then went happy in heart to his tapovan or hermitage.

Meantime, while Shivakocharyar was engaged in all these activities, Thinnan was busy hunting and killing animals to offer as food for his Lord. Just as before he roasted and cooked the flesh of the animals, added honey to the meat and packed it in the bark of the teak. He then took water in his mouth and flowers stuck in his hair and carrying the food packet and his bow and arrows climbed the mountain and reached the place of the *Shivalinga*.

He found someone had already poured water and placed flowers on Shiva's head. His hands were not free so with his feet he pushed away the flowers. He then performed the ritual of *abisheka* in his own way by spitting the water from his mouth on Shiva's head and placed the flowers reverently on His head. His face was glowing with happiness; as he sat down to offer the meat delicacy he had so lovingly prepared. As he placed it before the Lord he said that the meat he had brought was tastier than the meat he had offered yesterday. "I have tasted and tested every piece before offering it to you my Lord — also I have added honey to make it sweet." As darkness fell, he took his stand beside the *Shivalinga* to keep guard.

Nagan and Thathai after hearing what Nanan and Kadan had to say about the condition of Thinnan came to mount Kalahasti and to the place where Thinnan was standing vigil. In spite of all their entreaties, they could not sway Thinnan from his purpose. They went away feeling very sad and helpless.

Thinnan spent the night watching over the Lord without even blinking his eyes. When the daylight broke, he went on his food hunting mission.

After he left Sivakocharyar came with his water, flower and food offering for the Lord and again found the place strewn with meat and bones. As before, he cleaned the place, went to the river had his bath again, and after purifying the place with water sanctified by *mantra*s, performed his ritual worship — chanting the sacred *mantra* and Vedas. He prayed to Lord Shiva to put an end to these hideous happenings.

Lord Shiva was moved by Shivakocharyar's prayers and on the fifth day of the alternate worship by Sivakacharyar and Thinnan, he appeared in a dream to Sivakocharyar and spoke to him thus

> My dear devotee, do not think it is an ordinary hunter who is doing this. Listen to what I have to say about him. His whole body is an embodiment of love and devotion to me, his mind is always focused on me and all that he offers is very pleasing to me. When he removes the flowers you have placed upon me with his foot it gives me more joy than the touch of the foot of my beloved son Subramanya Kartikeya. The water he throws out of his mouth feels like the pure water from the Ganges. The flowers he places on my head from his hair are like fresh blooms with fragrance which cannot be equalled even by the flower offering of Brahma and other gods to me. As for the meat which he so lovingly chews and offers to me, it is more sweet than the *havir bhagam* offered to me during *Yaga*s. The sweetness of his talking to me without being aware of anyone else but me is more pleasing to me than the praises in verses sung by the great sages; I want you to see the devotion of this man. So tomorrow you should hide yourself behind me and watch him. Only then will you realize his greatness.

Thus spoke the Lord to Sivakocharyar and disappeared.

When Sivakocharyar woke up from this strange dream, the words of the Lord in praise of a low-born ignorant hunter, made him wonder with awe at the greatness of this man who surpassed even the gods in his devotion to the Lord! "What a sinner I am, worse than a diseased dog to have thought ill of such a man!"

On the morrow, Sivakocharyar early in the morning went to the river Ponmukali, had his bath, climbed the mountain and hid himself behind the *Shivalinga*.

Before Sivakocharyar reached there Thinnan had already left for his hunting. He returned ready with his water, flower and meat parcel, while coming he saw many bad omens like blood on the way. Thinnan was shattered "O, something has happened to my beloved master, my Lord, my Shiva" he cried. Thinnan ran all the way to the shrine. The merciful Lord who was indeed the servant of all his devotees, wanted to reveal to Sivakocharyar the extent of the devotion of Thinnan and so he caused his right eye to bleed. Thinnan came running to find the Lord's right eye oozing blood. The water which he held in his mouth for *abhisheka* spilled out, the meat rolled to the ground, and the flowers intended for worship fell from his hair. Like a puppet who falls when the string held by the puppeteer breaks, Thinnan slumped down with grief.

For some time he lay as if dead and eventually regaining consciousness, cried in anguish who had done this to his Lord? He took up his bow and arrows thinking that some of his tribesmen might have done it or some wild beast, not knowing where to find the culprits he searched all round the forest. Since he could not find any man or beast he came back and putting his arms round the *Shivalinga* cried out loud, shedding tears, "what can I do to alleviate this suffering of my lord? How can I stop the bleeding?" he walked back into the woods muttering, "I will bring the herbs that hunters use for healing their wounds." He went out and collected the medicinal herbs.

He pressed the juice on the bleeding eye but it had no effect, "what can I do? O God, my Shiva, show me the way," he cried.

Suddenly a proverb came to his mind "a limb for a limb." He jumped up and with his arrow he dug out his right eye and pressed it on the Lord's bleeding eye, to his immense joy the bleeding stopped at once. He jumped with uncontrolled happiness. A huge man that Thinnan was, he clapped his hand and danced with joy.

While he was celebrating, the Lord of Kalahasti made his left eye start bleeding. This was done for the benefit of instructing Sivakocharyar who was watching all this. Suddenly all the happiness went out of Thinnan, and he fell into a deep despondency. He however soon recovered as he now knew the remedy. He had only to take up an arrow and dig out the other eye and press it on the Lord's bleeding lift eye. He was lost in thought for a moment as it struck him that if he lost both eyes he would not know the location of the left eye. He therefore put his foot over the Lord's left eye and was going to pluck out his eye with his arrow when the Lord who did not want to test his devotee any further, called out in a resonant voice "Kannappa, stop" and held his hand with his own divine hand.

Brahma and all the gods and celestial beings showered the heavenly *karpaga* flowers and the air was filled with holy chants.

Sivakocharyar who was a stunned witness to all this came out and prostrated in front of the Lord, and embraced Thinnan. From that day Thinnan was known only as Kannappan and he took his place among the 63 Nayanars in the *Periya Puranam* as kannappa Nayanar.

3

Tirunalai Povaar Nayanar
Or the Story of Nandanar

ADANOOR was a village in Cholamandalam. Nandan belonged to the Pariah caste and lived in the paracheri far away from the brahmin village.

Pariahs worked as scavengers for the brahmin villages. They worked in the fields ploughing and sowing the land and also did the harvesting. Thus they were both landless agricultural labourers and the village scavengers. They were also traditional drummers and beat the *parai* (drum) at funerals. They were regarded as the lowest of the low and belonged to the untouchable community which had to observe physical and ritual distance from all the other castes.

Nandan had the grant of a small piece of land and earned his living from the proceeds from the land. He also carried on his own occupation, that of making skins for the percussion instruments to be played in the temples, and strings for the divine musical instruments the harp (*yazh*) and the *veena*. He also made *korochanam*, an incense for worship in the temple.

Nandan was an exceptional man, in that from childhood he was a devotee of the Lord Shiva. His mind, body and soul belonged to Shiva, no one else had a place in his heart except this Lord.

Nandan would go from place to place visiting the Shiva temples, he would stand at a respectful distance from the entrance far away from the *sanctum sanctorum* where the deity was, as he was an untouchable and could not enter the temple. He would sing in praise of Shiva and dance in ecstasy.

Once he visited the Shiva temple in Tiruppunkoor and stood in front of the entrance straining his neck and standing on his toes to have a glimpse of the Lord, but the Shiva *vahanam*, the divine vehicle of Shiva which was the Nandi bull on which the Lord rode, was right in front and obstructed his view. Nandan prayed that he should have a *darshana* of the Lord.

Shiva who called himself the servant of his devotees, immediately caused Nandi to move sideways so as to allow his Nandan to have a good *darshana*. Nandan was overwhelmed with devotion and love for his Lord and had his fill of the glorious vision of the *Shivalinga*. His eyes were streaming with tears of happiness and he danced in ecstasy. With great difficulty he tore himself away and retraced his footsteps homewards. As he left he saw the big pit that was created when Nandi moved away. He at once set to work and dug deep till he struck water and he made a tank there.

In a similar manner he visited many Shiva temples and left his mark there by rendering some humble service or the other towards the maintainance of the temple.

He had a longing in his heart to visit Tillai also known as Chidambaram where Lord Shiva abided as Nataraja, meaning the Lord of the cosmic dance. Chidambaram was the *Kanakasabha* (literally "golden auditorium") where Sabhapathy Lord Nataraja was lifting his left foot in the cosmic dance pose. One day his desire to go to Chidambaram was so intense that he lay awake the whole night, alternating between intense longing and deep despair. In the morning the thought came to him that even if he were to go to Chidambaram he would not be able to have his *darshana* as he was a Pariah and could not enter the temple. He felt very sad, but consoled himself that it was God's will. He also found it difficult to complete his intense toil in the landlord's field in time to make the pilgrimage to Chidambaram. He could not go despite his deep longing to do so. But the yearning to go to Chidambaram where Shiva was Nataraja, never left him. Everyday, he would tell himself that he would go the next day, in Tamil — *nalai poven,* meaning "tomorrow I will go." Still the stigma of his caste prevented him and his status as virtual serf on his landlord's field prevented him. He still wanted to go and he said to himself "*nalai poven* (I will go tomorrow)." If anyone asked him when he was going to Tillai he would say *nalai poven.* Thus days passed with his intent of *nalai poven* and that tomorrow never came. Nandan henceforth was called by the name "Tirunalai Povar," meaning "the one who will go tomorrow." Suddenly one day his landlord gave him permission to proceed and his desire was such that he did set out for Chidambaram, and made the journey by foot.

An oral tradition relating to Nandanar narrates a miraculous story with regard to his departure for Chidambaram. His landlord set him an impossible task and said that if he could sow the seeds, irrigate the fields and harvest the crops within a month, he could go to Chidambaram as per his desire. By the divine blessings of the Lord, the average fields of the landlord yielded a bumper harvest within a record time and that was how Nandanar could go to have the darshan of his beloved Shiva.

It took him many days to reach his destination. At last he reached Chidambaram. He crossed the outskirts and saw walls built all round the city with a gate in the centre. He entered the gate and locked in and saw a brahmin village where the sacred fires were lit and smoke spiralled to the skies. The chanting of Vedas could he heard in the distance. He hesitated to go in and made obeisance from where he was, and went round the city circumambulating it for many days and nights with the name of Shiva on his lips and devotion in his heart. He had at last reached the place where he longed to be.

He knew the temple of Nataraja was inside the orthodox village of Chidambaram and wanted to have *darshana* of his beloved Shiva. But how could he, an untouchable, enter? Such was the predicament of Nandanar. He knew that as a Pariah he had no right to pollute the sacred site by entering the temple. But how then could he have *darshana* of Him? "My caste stands in the way," he cried in sorrow and despair. With a heart heavy with sadness he at last lay down his weary body and slept on the outskirts of Chidambaram. Sabhapathy Nataraja appeared to him in a dream and told him "you should purify yourself by immersing yourself in a fire. You will then emerge from the fire unscathed as a brahmin. The brahmins will then have to accept you. You can then come to my *sannidhi* with the other brahmins." So saying, the lord blessed Nandan. That night he also appeared in the dreams of all the other brahmins and ordered them to make a big fire for his devotee Nandan.

Next morning the brahmins woke up and gathered in front of the temple. "Let us do as the Lord has bidden us," they said. They went to where Tirunalai Povar was and told him that the Lord Sabhapathy had in a dream asked them to build a big fire for him. "I am ready to obey the will of the Lord and the assembled brahmins," said Tirunalai Povar. The brahmins dug a pit and made a fire in front of the south *gopuram* (tower). They then informed Tirunalai Povar. Tirunalai Povar came to the fire pit, his mind wholeheartedly concentrated on the feet of Lord Shiva. He stepped into the fire and as soon as the flames engulfed him, the fire suddenly went out. Nandanar emerged as a saintly brahmin with the sacred thread of three strains, and long hair and flowing beard. When the brahmins assembled there saw this miracle they fell down and paid obeisance to the brahmin sage.

Tirunalaipovar was taken by the brahmins in a stately procession into the temple. He went with them, prostrated before the southern *gopuram* and went into the *sanctum sanctorum* of Kanakasabhapthy Lord Shiva. Reaching the *Shivalinga,* he suddenly merged into it in a blaze of light. The brahmins were amazed to find that he had disappeared from their sight. Seeing this wonderful miracle they sang in praise of the Lord and Tirunalai Povar. Thus Nandanar who was born an untouchable, was absorbed in the Lord and attained eternal bliss at the feet of Lord Nataraja. He enjoyed physical union with the divine, a blessing which no high born brahmin had been able to secure.

The devotion of Tirunalai Povar Nayanar — the Pariah Nandanar — is one of the most moving stories in the *Periya Puranam*.

4

Pusalar Nayanar

LONG, long ago in south India the Pallavas ruled over Thondaimandalam, with their capital at Kanjeepuram. The Pallava kings were famous for their architecture especially their rock-cut temples.

Tirunindravur is a place on the road from Kanjeepuram to Chennapattinam. It is at this holy place that the present story is located.

Pusalar was a brahmin devotee of Lord Shiva. He spent all his time in serving and attending to the needs of the devotees of Shiva. For a long time a desire was growing in him to build a temple for his beloved Lord. He knew exactly how he would build it, the plans and architectural designs were clearly visualized in his head. He went about trying to collect funds for this ambitious project since his mind was set on building the temple. However, hardly any donations were forthcoming for fulfilling this noble desire. He therefore decided he would build this temple without stone, brick or lime. He would build the temple for his beloved Lord in his heart.

His plans were complete. He had collected mentally all the necessary material. The outer quadrangle (*prakaram*) which went right around the temple was built and the inner quadrangle leading to the *sanctum sanctorum* with pillars beautifully sculptured was completed. The roofs had floral designs and the walls depicted scenes showing the greatness of Shiva and his marriage to Parvati. His children Ganapathy and Karthikeya had separate shrines.

The high *gopuram* (tower) was magnificent. It had taken him a long time to complete this huge temple. Now it remained only to fix an auspicious date and time to install the *Shivalinga* with all pomp and splendour, with the rituals of Vedic chanting, mingled with the music of *mangala-vadyams*, i.e. auspicious musical instruments such as the *veenai* and the *nadaswaram*.

He looked into the almanac and fixed an auspicious date and time for the installation. Strangely the Pallava King Kadarajan had also built a temple for Lord Shiva in Kanchipuram. He had also fixed the same date and time as Pusalar had for the installation of the *Shivalinga*.

The previous night of the installation Lord Paramashiva appeared in a dream to the king and said "In Tirunindravur there is a brahmin, a great devotee of mine named Pusalar who has built a temple for me. I will have to be present there when he installs me in the *garbha graha* (*sanctum sanctorum*). Therefore you must change your installation to another day," so saying he disappeared.

The king woke up and made preparation to go to Tirunindravur where Pusalar had built a temple for Lord Shiva. He enquired of the people in Tirunindravur about a new temple built by one Pusalar for which the installation of the *Shivalinga* and *kumbhabhishekam* of the *gopuram* was to be done that day. But everyone he asked denied having any knowledge of any new temple. No one had built any temple here they said.

The king then approached some brahmins and asked them "Who is Pusalar?" They told him that he was a learned brahmin of the place. "We will bring him to you, your majesty," they said and were about to go, when the king stopped them and said "no, I will come with you to see him." He saw Pusalar sitting in deep meditation. Hearing the noise of a multitude of people, Pusalar opened his eyes and saw a crowd and the king himself standing in front of him. The king with folded hands said, "Swami, the Lord Parameshvara came to me in a dream and told me that you have built a temple for him and that you are going to install the *Shivalinga* and perform *kumbhabhisheka* to the goburam today and He has asked me to postpone my installation to another day."

Pusalar was stunned. His heart overflowed with happiness. "O! My Lord has blessed me." He cried in joy. He addressed the king thus: "O king, my temple for my beloved Lord is in my heart. Since I had no funds and no means to build a temple for Him which was my intense desire, I have mentally built a temple for Him in my heart and today the auspicious hour is nearing for the installation of the *Shivalinga*." Saying thus, he went into a state of blissful *samadhi* or meditation.

The king fell down and prostrated before him and left for his capital.

Pusalar then, as scheduled, installed the *Shivalinga* in the *sanctum sanctorum* of his heart and performed the *kumbhabhishekam* amid Vedic chanting and music from the *mangalavadyam*s.

Thus Pusalar joined the illustrious line of Nayanars and became known as Pusalar Nayanar. He worshipped Shiva who dwelled in the temple of his heart for many years and reached the feet of the Lord.

It is recorded in history that the Pallava king built a Shiva temple at the place where Pusalar sat and meditated, now called Tiruninravoor, or the place where the Lord stood.

5

Karaikal Ammaiyar

THERE lived in the sea-port town of Karaikal a rich merchant named Dhanadattan. He had a daughter, his only child whom he named Punithavathi.

Punithavathi was a comely child and showed promises of growing up into a beauty. She was different from other children in that even from her infancy she was a devotee of Lord Shiva and would lisp His name in devotion.

In due course in accordance with the times Dhanadattan arranged her marriage with Paramadattan the son of Nithipathy a very rich merchant prince of Nagai or Nagapattinam.

Nithipathy came with his retinue, consisting of his son and family and relations to Karaikal, carrying gifts for the bride. With pomp and splendour, the marriage of Punithavathi with Paramadattan was solemnized.

As Punithavathi was his only child, Dhanadattan did not want her to go away from him and asked Paramadattan to stay on in Karaikal. He built a large house for them, and gave a portion of his wealth to them.

Punithavathi and Paramadattan lived very happily. Punithavathi was a good housewife and attended to all the needs of her husband. Paramadattan expanded his business with the capital his father-in-law had given him.

In the midst of all her domestic duties, Punithavathi did not in any way lessen her devotion to Shiva. She prayed to Him and worshipped Him with great devotion. She also served the Shiva devotees and pilgrims who came to her house, feeding them and giving them gifts, clothes and money.

One day, in the course of business, some people who were happy at the conclusion of a deal transacted with Paramadattan, gave him two big ripe mangoes supposed to be a rare variety. Paramadattan sent the fruits home to Punithavathi. Punithavathi kept them for serving her husband in his midday meal.

Just then a venerable old man who claimed that he was a devotee of Shiva came to the door of Punithavathi's house and asked for food saying he was very hungry. Punithavathi with great devotion brought him water to wash his feet and invited him inside. She placed a mat for him to sit. The vegetables for the afternoon meals were not yet prepared but there was hot rice which was first cooked. She served him the rice with ghee and brought one of the mangoes for him to eat with the rice. The Shiva devotee hungrily ate his food and enjoyed the delicious mango fruit. He blessed Punithavathi and took his leave, accepting the costly gifts she gave him.

Paramadattan came home from work, had his bath and sat down for his meals. Punithavathi served him food with the choicest vegetable dishes. Having eaten heartily he asked his wife to bring him the mango fruit he had sent home. Punithavathi brought the remaining fruit and served it. Paramadattan enjoyed the sweetness of the fruit and asked her to bring the other fruit also.

Punithavathi began to tremble with fear. How could she tell her husband that she had given away one fruit to a Shiva devotee? Her husband's one major fault was his extremely suspicious nature. She closed her eyes and prayed to her Lord Shiva to save her. Shiva was a god who was easily moved by a devotee's prayer. He was so kindhearted that he immediately came to her rescue. Lo and behold! She found a magnificent yellow mango fruit in her palm. She took it to her husband. He bit into the fruit and soon finished it. He found it so sweet and delicious it was unlike any fruit he had ever had before and much tastier than the one he had just eaten. He called Punithavathi and asked her bluntly, "This fruit is a heavenly fruit. Surely, it is not possible that such a fruit can be found on this earth. Be truthful and tell me how you got it?" Punithavathi was in a dilemma. She did not want to tell a lie. At last she decided to tell the truth and face the consequences of his wrath. She told her husband about the Shiva devotee who was hungry and wanted food. As the vegetables were not yet ready, she served him rice and to go with it served him one mango. "When you asked for the second mango, I prayed to Lord Shiva to save me and he gave me this fruit," she confessed. Paramadattan was amazed and did not quite believe her and wanted to test her, so he asked her to get him another such fruit from her Lord Shiva to prove herself. Once more. Punithavathi went inside and prayed to her god — her Shiva — to give her another mango fruit. "If you do not," she told Shiva, "my husband will think I am a liar, O Shiva, save me from ignominy." She prayed with tears flowing from her eyes. Again she found a magnificent fruit in her hand and joyfully she gave it to her husband. He took it in his hand wondering at the miracle and lo! the fruit disappeared.

Paramadattan was shaken with awe and fear; he realized that his wife was no ordinary woman but a divine being. From that day he treated his wife with great respect and did not touch her. For him she was not his wife but a goddess to be worshipped. He did not want to live with her anymore. He quietly asked his servants to fit up a ship with enough provisions to last a few months. As he was a sea-merchant and went on sea-voyages for trade, he took leave of Punithavathi and left with some fishermen on a long voyage.

Paramadattan went to distant sea-ports for trade, and eventually went to Nagapattinam. He lived there, married a merchant's daughter and became a prosperous trader. In course of time his wife gave birth to a daughter whom he named Punithavathi after his first wife. He thought of Punithavathi as a divine goddess and therefore named his daughter after one whom he had begun to regard as his *kula deivam*.

All this time Punithavathi was blissfully ignorant of her husband's whereabouts. She was under the impression that he was gone on a long voyage for trade, and carried on her household duties as a virtuous housewife. Some of her kinsmen came to know that Paramadattan had settled down in Nagapattinam and was prospering as a trader. They decided to take Punithavathi with them and unite her with her husband.

The whole party travelled in a caravan with Punithavathi accompanying them and after several days of travel reached the city where Paramaddattan was living. They sent an emissary to his house informing him about Punithavathi's arrival. Paramadattan with his second wife and daughter hastened to meet her.

As soon as he saw the lovely divine lady he fell at her feet and said, "Devi, by your grace I am doing well. This is my wife and this is my daughter whom I have named Punithavathi after you." All three prostrated before her.

Paramadattan told everyone present, "I worship her as Devi, all of you also bow to her and get her blessings."

How did Punithavathi react? How did she take this? Her intense devotion to Lord Shiva gave her the strength to bear the loss of her husband, who had married another. She loved her husband and must have been stunned by his statement — her mind and heart immediately turned to Lord Shiva and she prayed with intense fervour to Him that she should be rid of this beautiful body. Shiva granted her wish and she was transformed into a skeletal form, fearful to behold — a form which would be worshipped by the people on earth and by the heavenly beings.

Everyone was dumbstruck by this miracle and chanting the name of Shiva made their obeisance to her and left. Punithavathi whose heart was already full of love and devotion for Shiva broke into verse and composed the famous Thiru Anthadhi and the twin garlands of verses in praise of Kailasanatha.

She desired to go to Mount Kailasa, and with speed faster than the speed of the mind she reached Mount Kailasa.

To reach the peak where Kailasanatha resided she decided to walk on her head as she did not wish to trample on the sacred ground. Seeing a skeleton with head down and legs up the minions of Uma Devi, the consort of Kailasapathi ran to inform her of this spectacle. Wanting to hear from the lips of her husband the greatness of this devotee, Uma Devi requested Shiva to narrate to her the life of this Saint.

Paramashiva then said, "know then that the saint who is coming here is a very great devotee of mine — my *ammaiyar* (my mother). She requested me to give her this skeletal form." When Punithavathi as a skeleton reached near Shiva and Parvati, Shiva wanting the heavens and the whole universe to hear him, addressed her as *ammaye* (mother). Punithavathi in response called Shiva *appa* (father) and fell at his feet. The

Lord said to her, "ask of me any boon you desire," to which Karaikal Ammaiyar replied, "O Lord, grant that I may never be born again on earth. I also desire that when you, Deva, dance your cosmic dance, let me be at your feet, enjoying your dance and singing hymns in praise of you."

The Lord, full of compassion and love, directed her to go south to Alangkadu, saying, "Be there with me when I dance and play the cymbals for me." So saying, he blessed her.

Punithavathi henceforth to be known as Karakial Ammaiyar walked her way back on her head to Alangkadu.

She witnessed the dance of Shiva and sang the immortal hymn Kongaithirangai, a Tirupadhikam and the entire group of songs known as Tiruvalangattu Mootha Tirupadhikam.

Karaikal Ammaiyar·can be seen sitting very near the lifted leg of the dancing Shiva enjoying the bliss of devotion in most scultural representations of her in Tamil temples including the celebrated Nataraja temple at Chidambaram.

Part II

Later Saints

6

Sridhara Venkateswara Ayyaval

In this *Kali-yuga* there have been many saints who have manifested and left their footprints on the sands of Time. Through their intense devotion to God they have wrought many miracles and proved that the path to *moksha* was not by ritualistic worship but by pure devotion, chanting and singing the names of God.

In pre-modern times, India was broken up into small kingdoms ruled by Chitrarasar or petty chieftains. Maheshapuram was a small kingdom ruled by King Partibhan. His chief minister was a very wise and learned brahmin named Sridhara Padmanabhan, popularly compared to Vashishtar and Agasthiar in knowledge by the inhabitants of that little kingdom. The king asked his advice on every issue and acted accordingly. The king bestowed lands and houses to him and treated him generously.

Sridhara Padmanabhan and his wife Sundari had everything but they had no child. They went daily to the temple of Lord Dakshinamurthy and prayed to him to bless them with a child. By the grace of Lord Dakshinamurthy a son was born to Sundari. The birth of the child fulfilled their desire for an heir. The child was given the name Sridhara Venkateswara, but was lovingly called by his parents and everyone else as Ayya.

As the boy grew up, everyone was charmed by his grace and beauty. At the right age he was sent to the *pathashala*. He

1. Sridhara Venkateswara Ayyaval.

was a boy who loved learning and very soon he mastered all that the *gurus* taught him. He was an unusual boy. He loved to listen to the stories of great saints. He knew the Shastras and Upanishads thoroughly and loved to sing the names of gods in musical form. These devotional compositions are called bhajans. After his *upanayanam* — that is his initiation with the sacred thread as a *brahmachari* — Ayya recited the Gayatri *mantra* regularly. Sridhara Venkateswara was now of marriageable age and his parents arranged his marriage with a beautiful and equally pious girl. Ayya's father had great plans for his son. He wanted him to take over the chief ministership of the state after him.

But Ayya had already chosen his path, a life dedicated to God. In that his wife was of an equal bent of mind. Both of them spent their days in singing bhajans and worshipping God with intense devotion.

Ayya's father was very disappointed and tried his best to make his son get interested in state affairs. One day Ayya decided to make it clear to his parents that he was not interested in any office and had dedicated his life to the service of God. "Father, when I have the wealth that is Lord Parameshvara, a wealth which will never diminish, what need have I to work for wealth and power which is inconsistent?" he said. And he expounded the philosophy of the wealth to be gained from worship of the Lord Chandramauli to his father. It was a discourse so profound that Sridhara Padmanabhan was astounded at the knowledge of his son. Ayya was a gift of Lord Dakshinamurthy, so he belonged to him, he consoled himself. And from then on he and his wife participated and enjoyed the divine musical bhajans of their son Sridhara Venkateswara.

Years rolled by, Ayyaval's aged parents also passed away. Now all earthly bonds were severed and Sridhara Venkateswara Ayyaval was a free bird to soar away anywhere he liked.

As soon as the king heard of the death of Sridhara Padmanabhan, he came to the house to offer his condolence and straightaway asked Sridhara Venkateswara Ayyaval to take over the chief ministership. But Ayyaval firmly refused the offer and begged of the king to let him go his own way. The king was moved and asking Ayyaval's forgiveness returned to his palace.

Ayyaval's fame had spread to all corners of Tamil Nadu. Oblivious of name or fame Ayyaval continued his worship of Shiva, singing divine songs composed by him at community *bhajans*. With the wealth his father had left him, he fed the poor and kept an open house for all devotees of God. People who saw him thought that perhaps he himself was Lord Paramashiva, so powerful and striking was his appearance. He would be immersed in meditation on the Lord for hours, and when awake would sing songs in praise of Shiva and dance in ecstasy, his hands beating tune with the brass cymbals or *jalara* as it is called.

The news of Ayyaval's greatness spread it seemed as if it was carried by the wind to all corners, and the king also heard about it. He was eager to see this great son of Sridhara Padamanabhan and one day quietly incognito came to the house of Ayyaval. At that time Ayyaval was in a state of deep samadhi (meditation) oblivious to his surrounding.

But the local people who were there recognized the king and said loudly — loud enough to disturb his *samadhi* — "Our Prabhu has come." Because of the loud noise he was disturbed from his deep meditation and for a moment thought, "O! Prabhu must be my Prabhu Chandramouleeswarar" and opened his eyes and looked around. When he did not find his Prabhu, he became red eyed with sadness and disappointment mixed with anger. He asked, "where is my Prabhu?" Ignorant as they were, the people surrounding him, pointed at the king and said, "here is your Prabhu."

Sridhara Ayyaval was now angry with himself for expecting to see his Prabhu when he was always with him within his heart, "O fool that I am seeing the Lord in my mind's eye all the time and still wish to see his outward form." This was why he had to undergo this agony! He then sang a *shloka* describing the form of Shiva with his consort Parvati wherein he said, "Shiva, the friend of the poor and helpless — he is my Prabhu not this king Partibha." This recurrent refrain ended the *shloka*. The people stood in silent awe of the greatness of this saint. The king came forward and humbly begged Ayyaval's forgiveness for coming unannounced which had caused this confusion and returned to his palace.

Thus, Ayyaval's days were spent blissfully in prayer and devotion to Lord Shiva. One day, he decided that the time had come for him to renounce everything — every worldly possession he had — and go on a pilgrimage to as many of the Shiva *kshetra*s he could go. His wife who was not in any way lesser than him in her piety and devotion readily agreed to go with him.

Sridhara Ayyaval then proceeded to distribute his large wealth to the poor and needy. He gave away everything he had, and with the *dhoti* he was wearing and a brass vessel for begging for food he and his wife set out. When the king heard Ayyaval was leaving this place he came and prostrated before him and sought his blessings. Sridhara Ayyaval blessed the king with all his heart and left his home to visit other sacred places. It is said that it was during this pilgrimage that Ayyaval composed many of the poetry and *kritis* attributed to him.

Most important of the places he visited were Tiruchipuram (now Tiruchirapalli), Srirangam, Jambukeswaram, and other places. He composed *Jambunatha Ashtakam* — a *shloka* containing eight stanzas and *Mathrubutha Sathakam* — a hundred stanzas *shloka*. After a long sojourn in these places, he came to Tanjore.

At that time Tanjore (Thanjavur) was ruled by Sahaji Maharaja. Tanjore was the centre for culture — scholars, musicians, philosophers, and artists were all attracted to this seat of arts and music. Sridhara Ayyaval found an affinity in this atmosphere of scholars.

He decided to settle down in a village nearby called Tiruvisainallur. The Lord had decided to make him live the life of a brahmin householder.

Sridhara Ayyaval took up residence there and earned his food by daily *Uncha-vritti* that is going round the villages singing *bhajans* and standing before every doorstep where the lady of the house would come out go round him three times and after prostrating before him, empty the contents of a plate of raw rice into his vessel. Thus Sridhara Ayyaval spent his days getting up early in the morning and after a bath would first visit Lord Karkadeswarar. There he would complete his meditation and mantra japa and go the rounds for *Uncha-vritti* (begging for food) that would be his bodily exercise. His wife would cook the rice he brought and with whatever she made he would have his midday meal and rest for a little while. Every evening without fail he would cross the river Kaveri and visit the Mahalinga temple in Tiruvidaimaruthur. He did not miss the worship for even a single day.

The protection of the king who upheld *dharma*, the

intellectual and spiritual delight of conversing with scholars and poets and the sheer beauty of the perennially flowing river Kaveri captivated Sridhara Ayyaval. He happily settled into his daily routine. The people of the village looked up to him in all matters of religion and scriptures which needed to be elucidated. While he was there he composed voluminous religious poetry — like *Akhya Shashti, Dhaya Sathakam, Sthuthi Paddhati, Shiva Bhakti Kalpalathika, Shiva Bhakta Lakshanam, Arthihara Stothram, Dosha pariharashtakam,* etc. These writings flowed from his scriptural as well as spiritual knowledge and enlightened the world. The name of Shiva was on his lips ceaselessly.

These gems of compositions by Ayyaval reached the ears of Sahaji Maharaja. It was the nine-day festival of *Navaratri*. In the durbar hall of the palace, in the presence of the king, scholars would discuss and argue on many learned topics. The *maharaja* would also generously award the scholars with costly gifts.

The villagers of Tiruvisainallur where Ayyaval lived got together and decided to help him, as they were pained to see Ayyaval begging for his food daily with no other means of livelihood. They knew he would not accept anything from anybody not even from the *maharaja*, so they wanted to get a gift of a house and some farming land from the *Maharaja* so that Ayyaval would not have to go for *Uncha-vritti*. They felt that this was the only way they could repay their debt of gratitude to this great saint.

With this plan in mind they went to Ayyaval's house, and told him that they were all going to the *Navaratri durbar* where the *Vidvat Sabha* was taking place every day. Many eminent scholars had come from distant places and the discussions would be worth listening to. "You as a scholar would find it very interesting, so please come with us," they pleaded with one voice. Ayyaval agreed and went with them to Tanjore.

When they reached Tanjore, the *durbar* had just started. The scholars and poets who came there were all holding a coconut in their hands and some *mantra akshatai* that is raw rice coloured yellow which is used for blessing by elders. This was the custom also during the *Navaratri durbar* where the scholars blessed the king and gave the coconut and rice to him before taking their seats. When Ayyaval's turn came the brahmins also asked him to do likewise. Ayyaval said, *mama hridaye jagathathiko raja sekhrarosthi* meaning "In my heart the lord of the Universe Rajasekhar is present." "I owe no obligation to anyone nor do I serve any king. My gracious Lord the consort of Parvati is my master and I am his slave. I came here to listen to learned discourses and not to accept the gifts or patronage of the *maharaja*." When the assembled people heard him they were aghast. Ayyaval sat down, and prepared to listen to the learned discussions with full attention.

Whenever there was any discrepancy or a fault in the presentation Ayyaval would boldly point it out and corroborate it with convincing facts. The way he analysed and cleared the doubts of many amazed the scholars there. The *maharaja* who was a scholar himself was drinking in the honey-like flow of wisdom from this great savant.

The *Navaratri* festival got over, and on the last day the *maharaja* distributed largesse to all the *pundits* who had come. He was eagerly looking for Ayyaval to hand over to him costly gifts to his heart's content but Ayyaval was not in the least bothered about the gifts. As the last speaker sat down, he got up, threw his *angavastra* over his shoulder and walked his way back to Tiruvirsainallur.

The *pundits* who had accompanied Ayyaval from Tiruvisainallur saw him leave and went to the *maharaja* and pointing out Ayyaval said, "Your Highness, that man who is leaving the *durbar* hall is from our village. He has been in our village only for a short time, but he is a great scholar and a saint. He and his wife live on the food he gets by *Uncha-vritti*. If it pleases your Highness we request you to grant him a house and a bit of paddy land for his livelihood, so that he will not have to beg for his food. But Ayyaval will not accept anything from anybody. If he comes to know this is a gift bestowed on him he will leave our village, so if you give the *patta* in his name we will somehow see that he gets the benefit," they assured the *maharaja*.

Sahaji Maharaja had already noticed Ayyaval and was only too glad to give a house and paddy land as *patta* in his name.

After some days Ayyaval was told by the owner of the house in which he lived that it requires some repairs and he could move over to another house of his. So Ayyaval and his wife moved into his own house without knowing it was his. The villagers then requested him to teach the boys of the village lessons in Sanskrit and Veda *mantras*. He readily agreed, and as a *guru-dakshina* the proceeds from his land were given to him. Thus Ayyaval was taken care of by the people of Tiruvisainallur.

Now, it is a well known fact that God tests those whom he loves most. The lives of saints like the Alwars and Nayanars tell us about the great sufferings and tests they underwent before God finally accepted them as true devotees. The rough form of gold has to be cured in fire before its true lustre comes out as pure yellow gold. A sculptor has to use a sharp iron chisel to shape his image before it becomes a piece of art — so also Sridhara Ayyaval's testing time came.

One day, it was the *shraddham* ceremony (death anniversary) of his revered father. Ayyaval had invited three brahmins to partake of the food offered to Shiva, Brahma and Vishnu on *shraddham* days. He then gave his wife all the required provisions for cooking food for the brahmins, and went to the river Kaveri for his bath before starting the *shraddham* ceremonies. It was nearly 12 noon and the sun's heat was unbearably hot. Mother earth was scorching under the heat. Ayyaval was walking fast, when he heard someone calling "Ayyare Ayyare" in a plaintive voice. Ayyaval stood still trying to locate from where the sound came. From a nearby bush a famished form appeared. The man's stomach was so hollow that it looked as if it was sticking to his back, looking at him one could at once know that here was a man who must have been starving for days.

This starving beggar fell at Ayyaval's feet and said "I have not eaten anything for many days, you have appeared before me like God, please give me some food and save me," he sobbed. Ayyaval's heart melted with pity. He did not hesitate or have a second thought but asked the man to wait for a little while and promised him that he would bring him food.

He reached his house in a few minutes and took a portion of all that was cooked for the three brahmins in a big vessel and hurrying back gave the vessel to the beggar. The starving man just gobbled up the food, drank the water Ayyaval had brought along with the food and with a heart full of gratitude thanked Ayyaval and went on his way.

Ayyaval felt his ancestors themselves had come in the man's form and eaten the food, and he was happy and pleased. He returned home and asked his wife to clean the place and cook afresh for the invited brahmins.

But somehow the news of Ayyaval feeding a low caste beggar the food cooked for the *shraddha* ceremony had spread throughout the village. The brahmins of that village only knew the path of *karma* — they believed in rituals without engaging the heart in them. They knew nothing of *bhakti-yoga* and the *lila*s of God — the spiritual path where everyone high or low were God's children.

The brahmins of the village got together and discussed Ayyaval's action causing self-pollution by serving a low caste (perhaps even untouchable) beggar. They decided that he should be declared an outcaste and sent away from the village. This same Ayyaval whom they revered, who they respected as a great scholar and under whom they learnt the sacred texts, was now, within a few hours time, declared polluted and unfit to live among them only because he fed a hungry starving soul.

How can these ignorant brahmins know of the ways of God! A beggar or a brahmin, rich or poor, healthy or sick, it was all God's doing — He was the *sutradhara* (the great manager, literally one who holds all the threads of the story together) directing the people to be what they are!

In the meanwhile, Ayyaval unaware of all this, returned after a bath in the river, ready to perform the *shraddha* ceremony for his father. When he came back, he saw a crowd in front of his house. Being a wise man he at once understood the reason for this gathering. He also saw the three brahmins who were the special invitees representing Brahma, Vishnu and Shiva, to partake of the ceremonial food. He addressed the crowd thus, "O learned men, why have you congregated here at this time? Whatever it is, let me complete my duty in performing the *shraddha* ceremony of my father and I will answer all your questions. Let the three brahmin invitees please come forward and come into my house."

The brahmins rose angrily in one voice and said, "Swami, today is an important day for you. It is the *shraddha* ceremony of your departed father, but what have you done? You have given the food cooked for the brahmins to a *chandala*, a low caste beggar. Unless you undergo a purification ritual none of us will enter your house."

Sridhara Ayyaval was taken aback, and for a minute he closed his eyes in prayer. When he opened his eyes, his decision had been made. His face brightened. With folded hands he bowed his head before the brahmins and said, "Let the *shraddha* ceremony be over now, we will discuss this matter later," so saying he went in and bolted the door. The people assembled there were astonished at his calm demeanour and at what he said.

How is he going to perform the *shraddha* without the three brahmins who will represent Brahma, Rudra and Vishnu? "Let us see how he can," and the people sat there in a mocking attitude.

Sridhara Ayyaval was no ordinary man. Shiva resided in his heart. He went inside and for half an hour sat in deep meditation. He then got up and spread three plantain leaves — one for Vishvadeva, one for his father, and one for Maha-Vishnu.

He took *dharba* grass and invoking Brahma, made him sit at the leaf of Vishvadeva, he then invoked Rudra (Shiva) and made him sit at the leaf meant for his father and at the third leaf he invoked Maha-Vishnu to partake of the food. He started repeating the *Shraddha mantra*s as prescribed by the Shastras, his wife served the several items of food prepared, on the plantain leaves, while he completed the *homa* (*havan*) offering of *ghee* in the fire.

The three celestial brahmins had their fill of the feast. The people who were sitting outside clearly heard the brahmins blessing the *karta* or the person who performed the *shraddha*. They looked at each other with disbelief. The learned fools who were there could not grasp the significance of this miracle. How could they know the greatness of a devotee? Did not Mandana Misra invoke the sages Jaimini and Vyasa as brahmins when he performed the *shraddha* for his ancestors? Have they heard the story of Jnanadeva invoking the divine trinity Shiva, Brahma and Vishnu as brahmins for the *shraddha* ceremony? Likewise Ayyaval who was no less a devotee had invoked the divine trinity as brahmins. What cannot a true devotee achieve?

The *shraddha* ceremonies were over and the door of Ayyaval's house opened. There was still a ritual left, that of immersing the *pinda* of rice balls in the river. As he came out, the brahmins confronted him and said "You have by your magical powers managed to complete the *shraddha* invoking whom we do not know — as far as we know no brahmin has come out of your house this way. So even if you are a tantric and have magical powers unless you undergo the *prayaschitta* (purification rites) we impose on you, we will not accept you in this village, and you cannot live here." Hearing this Ayyaval with a smile said, "O good men, there is still one more ritual I have to perform tomorrow morning, after that I will accept any decision of yours regarding what *prayaschitta* I should undergo."

The next day the sun rose, all the brahmins congregated at Ayyaval's house. Sridhara Ayyaval bowed to them, "What *prayaschitta* have you decreed for me?" he asked them. Since they had already come to a decision they said, "Swami, you have to purify yourself by having a bath in the holy Ganges. Nothing short of that can expiate you of your sin."

The river Ganges flows from the Himalayas to the plains in north India. In ancient times pilgrims from the south had to undertake this hazardous journey of 2000 miles walking all the way unless they were rich enough to travel by carts or palanquins. Many who went, never returned, some died on the way and did not reach Benaras or Kashi as it is called. So the clever brahmins were aiming at the death penalty for Ayyaval by decreeing that he should go to Kashi. But Ayyaval agreed.

As these events were happening here, in Tiruvidaimaruthur which lay across the river Kaveri, in the temple of Mahalinga, the temple priest opened the *garbha-griha* (*sanctum sanctorum*) for getting the Lord ready for the evening *puja*. He was amazed to see the Lord had thrown off the cloth with which the priest had clothed Him in the morning and everything else with which the priests had decorated Him including flower garlands and sandalwood paste. He was wearing a new *dhoti*, sandalwood paste and *tulsi* leaves. As the priest looked speechless not understanding how this could have happened, he heard a voice saying "O Archakar, this afternoon I was invited by Tiruvisainallur Sridhara Venkateswara to take food in his house on the occasion of the *shraddha* ceremony of his father. Having partaken of food there, I cannot have any other food tonight as I should fast; therefore do not offer *naivedyam* for me nor the evening *arati*." Hearing this the Archakar's eyes were filled with tears of devotion and he prayed to Lord Mahalinga and went away.

The next day while he was removing the *dhoti* and preparing the Lord for *abhisheka* the Archakar found on the head of the *linga* betel leaves, betel nuts, *tulsi* leaves and a coin — this is usually given as *dakshina* to brahmins. The Archakar was wonderstruck at seeing this miracle. What *lila*s can God not perform for his devotees!

The next day, Sridhara Ayyaval, after the *shraddha*, made his usual visit to Tiruvidaimaruthur to worship Lord Mahalinga. The Archakar asked him, "Yesterday was there a *shraddha* in your house? Is that why you missed your daily visit to the temple?" Ayyaval was surprised, "how did you know it was my father's *shraddha* yesterday?" he asked. The Archakar told him all that had happened, how Lord Mahalinga Himself told him about the *shraddha* and that He had been invoked to partake of the food as Rudra — and about the *dakshina* he had discovered that morning.

Ayyaval went into an ecstatic state of devotion and with tears streaming down his face, he sang the praises to the Lord and went home.

He narrated these extraordinary events to his wife and went to sleep, but kept tossing about, his mind troubled with the *prayaschitta* the brahmins had decreed. Towards early morning he must have dozed off, and he had a dream — Ganga Devi herself appeared and in a loving tone addressed him, "O *bhakta* Shikhamani (literally, the crown jewel among devotees), as per the decree pronounced on you by the villagers, there is no need for you to go to Kashi for a dip in the Ganga. The world should know your devotion to God. Therefore wherever the villagers want you to bring the Ganges water there will I be." So saying, she disappeared.

Sridhara woke up from his dream and his heart was filled with joy. How blessed he was that Shiva and Shakti both have come to his rescue, he lost himself in contemplation of God.

The all-knowing Sun God peeped through the dawn into the village of Tiruvisainallur, as if eager to be a witness to the wonderful events that were going to take place there.

The villagers were also very keen to see the penitent Ayyaval on his way to Kashi, perhaps never to return. With triumph written large on their faces, they came in large numbers to Sridhara Ayyaval's house. "When are you leaving," they asked him. In reply Ayyaval asked them, "O good people of Tiruvisainallur, I have a request, as per your commands I am willing to purify myself in the Ganges, but must I go to Kashi for that? Can I not bring the Ganges here? Then not only I can purify myself, but all of us can purify ourselves and wash away our sins."

Because of one good man, the whole village will benefit by the Ganges coming here, thought the villagers, but not fully aware of the greatness of Sridhara Ayyaval they were also somewhat sceptical and said "What? The river Ganga come here! You are getting it here!" "Yes, yes," replied Ayyaval, "because I have your blessings, I am confident I can bring the sacred Ganga here." "But in what way, and where exactly do you want me to bring her. This you must let me know" he concluded. The brahmins put their heads together and came out with the statement "Bring the Ganges from your own well, but the water should contain turmeric, *kumkum*, *karukumani* and other auspicious symbols, so that we will know it is real Ganga water." Sridhara Ayyaval told them to assemble near his well on the coming *amavasya* day (new moon day) adding "with your blessings I will bring the sacred Ganga here."

The news of this impending miracle spread to the other villages. Everyone was waiting for the wonderful event.

It was *amavasya*, the new moon day. A large crowd had gathered in the courtyard of Ayyaval's house and was jostling for space. A few prominent brahmins surrounded the well. Sridhara Venkateswara Ayyaval, his face shining with divinity, went round the well and closing his eyes, prayed to Ganga Devi to descend. On this occasion, he composed an eight stanza *shloka* in praise of Ganga Devi known as *Gangashtakam* on the spot and reciting it, waited with folded hands. As soon as he finished chanting the *Gangashtakam*, water overflowed from the well and flooded the whole area. In the water floated turmeric, *kumkum*, black beads, and the *picholai*, a ring made of palm leaf used during *Devi Puja*. The crowd was by now weeping and sobbing at this heavenly miracle and many were shouting "Hara, Hara, Mahadeva." The tears of the people mingled with the Ganges water, thus washing away their sins — it seemed the *prayaschitta* was for them not for Sridhara Ayyaval who was ever pure.

At that time the great Bodhendra Swamigal who was on a pilgrimage happened to reach Ayyaval's house just in time to witness this miracle. He saw the well overflowing with water and a divine person who looked like Lord Shiva himself standing there in *samadhi*, lost to the world around him. As soon as Bodhendra saw him he began to extol the greatness of Sridhara Ayyaval. Sri Ayyaval woke up from his state of samadhi and fell at the feet of Bodhendra praising him in a sloka. It was like the merging of three great spiritual sources — Sridhara Ayyaval, Srimad Bodhendra Desikendra, and the Ganga.

At this time a Gaur (or *Gowda*) brahmin from the north arrived there. He was carrying on his shoulders a Kavady (horizontal pole) with a pot on both sides. It was as if he knew that he would find the Ganges here. He filled the two pots with the Ganges water, and paid obeisance to the two saints. When he was about to leave, Bodhendra asked him, "Swami, where are you going?" The brahmin replied, "I was coming from Kashi with the two pots of Ganges water and was on my way to Rameswaram where they should be immersed in the sea. Last night I halted in Kumbakonam and in the night I had a dream in which Ganga Devi appeared and asked me to go to Sridhara Ayyaval's house in Tiruvisainallur. She told me, "You will find me there. Take the water from there and go to Rameswaram." She said this and disappeared. "I was surprised when in the morning I found both these pots empty. So I rushed here and as per Ganga Devi's command I am taking Ganges water from here." For the people of Tiruvisainallur who were already in a highly emotional state, this narration made them more remorseful and at the same time increased their devotion towards Ayyaval.

Bodhendra Swamigal spent many days with Sridhara Ayyaval singing *nama sankirtanam* and *bhajan*s and in giving discourses. It is rightly stated in the Vedas, Shastras and Puranas that in the *Kali-yuga* only *nama sankirtanam* is necessary to attain God's feet — there is no need for any ritualistic worship.

Bodhendra and Sridhara thus spent many happy days enjoying each other's company and the bliss of singing the divine name.

One day, Sri Bodhendra took out a bundle of all his writings — poems, songs, commentaries a colossal achievement. Likewise Sridhara took out his compositions and showed them to Bodhendra. Bodhendra was very happy to see these excellent writings but a thought passed through his mind, "all his writings are on Shiva." Sridhara Ayyaval read his mind and immediately sang a composition on Sri Rama — *Rama Pranama*. Bodhendra asked him, "how did you know what passed in my mind? I wanted to request you to compose 100 *shloka* on Hari, but this one *shloka* of yours is enough to prove your equal devotion to Hari and Shiva."

Sridhara Ayyaval has composed several *shloka*s in praise of Hari and Rama and others in the pantheon of gods. As a true son of God, *siddhis* or miracles came to him naturally. Like the great Tirujnana Sambandar he has even brought the dead to life.

Once, drought affected not only Tiruvisainallur but the whole districts of Tanjavur and Tiruchirapalli. Sridhara Ayyaval together with the villagers went to the river Kaveri and after a bath, each one filled up a pitcher of water. They all went to the temple of Karkadeswarar and performed *abhishekam* with the water. Ayyaval composed *Kulirashtakam* (for cooling). All the villagers recited this 108 times; by the time they finished, the heavens opened and torrential rains flowed.

Yet another time, too much rain which caused floods became a cause for concern. Sridhara could not cross the Kaveri to worship Lord Mahalinga at Tiruvidaimaruthur. Ayyaval was unhappy that he could not worship his Lord. At night Lord Mahalinga Himself in the form of the temple Archakar came in his dream and gave him Vibhuti Prasad and Ayyaval, as usual, gave the Archakar a coin as *dakshina*. Then Ayyaval asked him, "O, Archaka!, the river is swollen. How did you cross it and come to my home?" The Archakar replied, "I swam across."

Next morning when the Archakar removed the previous trappings he found a coin — it puzzled him. In the evening Ayyaval could cross the river as the water had receded and he came to the temple for worship. The Archakar asked Ayyaval "You could not come yesterday because of the heavy rains causing the river to be in spate, isn't it?" — Ayyaval replied, "but although I could not come you were kind enough to swim across and bring me the Vibhuti Prasad. I also gave you your usual *dakshina*." The Archakar was amazed at Ayyaval's devotion which made the Lord Himself go as the

Archakar and give him prasad. As for Sridhara Ayyaval, his heart was filled with gratitude and devotion for his beloved Lord Shiva.

Another very interesting incident is recorded in the life story of Ayyaval. In Tiruvisainallur itself there was a *mutt* called Kaveri Mutt. There one Sannyasi by name Govindasamyami lived. He was against the preaching of Sridhara Ayyaval and his propounding the theory that by *nama sankirtanam* alone, one can attain salvation or *moksha* and therefore there was no need of formalized worship. It was his contention that only women and shudras who were not authorised to recite the Gayatri *mantra* or the Vedic *mantra*s and were nor permitted any ritualistic worship, could use the path of *nama sankirtanam* to attain salvation.

Ayyaval never gave heed to his ramblings. One day while Govindasamyami was sleeping Lord Mahalingam appeared in his dream and said "Ada Papi! (literally, O, Sinner!) Why do you abuse my devotee? When the Shastras say that the only path to *moksha* in *Kali-yuga* is by *nama japa* and *nama sankirtanam*, who are you to say otherwise? Henceforth only *nama sankirtanam* is your path," and disappeared. Next morning the sannyasi came greatly agitated and fell at the feet of Sridhara and begged his forgiveness. Sridhara Ayyaval also bowed to him. It is said that Sadasivendrar also was a contemporary of Sridhara Ayyaval and was very much influenced by him, and later became a renowned composer.

In this way even though Sridhara Ayyaval made no difference in his worship of Shiva and Vishnu, the people wanted to test his devotion to Vishnu. On *Krishna Janmashtami* day (the birthday of Lord Krishna), they used the occasion to take out a procession of Lord Krishna through the village. When the procession reached Sridhara Ayyaval's house, he and his wife broke a coconut and offered *naivedyam* to Lord Krishna and reciting *Krishna Dvadasa Manjari* they prostrated in front of the Lord. Apart from this composition Ayyaval has composed *Dola Navaratna Malika* and *Achyutashtakam.*

Another time the European invaders came with a huge army and ravaged Cholamandalam. The people had prior information that they might be passing through Tiruvisainallur and the villagers came to Ayyaval for protection. Sridhara Ayyaval went with all of them to the river bank. They sat on the sands and were singing *bhajans*. The invaders came in a column on horse back. When they saw this huge crowd singing, something made the leader of the army get down from his horse and bow to Sridhara Ayyaval and he placed before him the loot he had plundered and asked his forgiveness and went away.

It is said that Ayyaval utilised that wealth for making a gem-studded gold *Nagabharanam* for Lord Mahalingeswara. There were numerous incidents like this in Ayyaval's life.

An important aspect of Ayyaval's life was his meeting with the child widow Avudai and her transformation into a self-realized saint under the spiritual guidance of her guru Sridhara Ayyaval. Avudai of Shencottai, was only eight years old when she was widowed. She was subjected to terrible suffering and made to shave off her hair and wear white, the mark of widowhood. She lived in the dark recesses of the house like a bat, afraid to come out because people regarded as inauspicious the very sight of a widow. When Sridhara Ayyaval visited Shencottai, the child widow fell at his feet and sobbed her heart out. Ayyaval, in the teeth of orthodox opposition, became her *guru* and guided her on the spiritual path. Avudai became "Avudai Akka," a renowned saint and went on to write many Vedantic works and mystical poems.

Time rolled on. Sridhara Ayyaval had the feeling that his days on earth were coming to an end. Meanwhile Sri Bodhendra had completed a pilgrimage to Rameswaram and was camping at the river bank in Vira Cholapuram. His desire now was to see his friend Sridhara Ayyaval, but God's dispensation was otherwise. On a full moon day while singing *nama sankirtanam* he went into a state of deep *samadhi* and this time the meditation was eternal. Bodhendra had attained the feet of Lord Vishnu, his *ishtadeva*. When Sridhara Ayyaval heard of the passing away of his friend Bodhendra he came in person and supervized the *maha samadhi*, rituals due to a great saint.

One day, as Sridhara Ayyaval was going to visit Lord Mahalingeswara temple he was so overcome by emotion that he sat near the Nandi platform and was singing bhajans. He then suddenly got up and went right inside the *garbha-griha*, that is the *sanctum sanctorum* and merged with his beloved Shiva.

The people waiting outside thought he had gone in to worship and would come out but they waited in vain. He never came out. The people then realized that he was one with God. They wept with joy and sorrow, joy because only now they understood his greatness and celebrated the saint who had lived in their midst as an ordinary householder. At the same time they experienced much sorrow because of their profound regret that they never fully realized his divinity. They made a resolution to practise his teachings and follow the path he had shown them.

Even today, in Tiruvisainallur in the house where Sridhara Venkateswara Ayyaval lived, every year in the month of Kartika (middle of November to middle of December) on *krishnapaksha panchami* — that is the fifth day after the full moon, his devotees congregate from far and wide and celebrate the great Sridhara Ayyaval's coming to live among them. The occasion is filled with musical discourses (*Hari kathas*), *Hari bhajans*, Vidvat Sabhas and music concerts. Everyone is fed sumptuously, all the days.

The festivities end solemnly on the *amavasya* (new moon), a day which comes a fortnight after the advent of the full moon. That was to commemorate the day Ayyaval merged with Lord Mahalinga. Since the exact day on which he merged was not known, the Kartika *amavasya* day when Sridhara Ayyaval brought the Ganges to his own well was fixed as the day they remembered his end. On that day *Anjaneya Utsava* is conducted and the fifteen-day celebrations brought to an end.

Thus lived and died the great Saint Sridhara Venkateswara Ayyaval. He was a saint luminary of the eighteenth century who occupies his rightful place with Bodhendra and Sadashiva Brahmendra within the *Hari bhajan sampradaya* of south India.

7

Sadashiva Brahmendrar

SADASHIVA Brahmendrar was an eighteenth-century saint. It was a golden era of saints and musicians. His contemporaries were Shri Bodhendra Swamigal and Shri Sridhara Venkateswara Ayyaval.

If Thyagarajar, Muthuswami Dhikshitar and Shyama Shastri were the Musical Trinity (they were also saints), Sadashivar, Bodhendra and Ayyaval were the Saintly Trinity (they were also composers).

Madurai is one of the most sacred and important cities of south India. It was the capital of the Pandyan Kingdom known as Pandyamandalam, a state that was ruled not by a man, but by a woman, Queen Meenakshi along with her consort Lord Shiva called Sundareshwar. In this famous city of Madurai, in a Telegu brahmin family, a son was born to Shri Somanatha Avadhanigal and Parvati. This son was later to be celebrated as Sri Sadashiva Brahmendrar. The period of his birth may be placed within 10 years of the beginning of the eighteenth century. His *guru* was Paramashivendrar. The name given to the boy was Sivaramakrishnan, and he was called by his pet name "Pichu."

As a child, Pichu was a very lively boy, but during his school days or *gurukala vasam* days, he was known as a serious student. Very studious, he very soon went far ahead of the other boys and quickly mastered the intricacies of Sanskrit grammar and Tamil. Learned *pundit*s were amazed at the

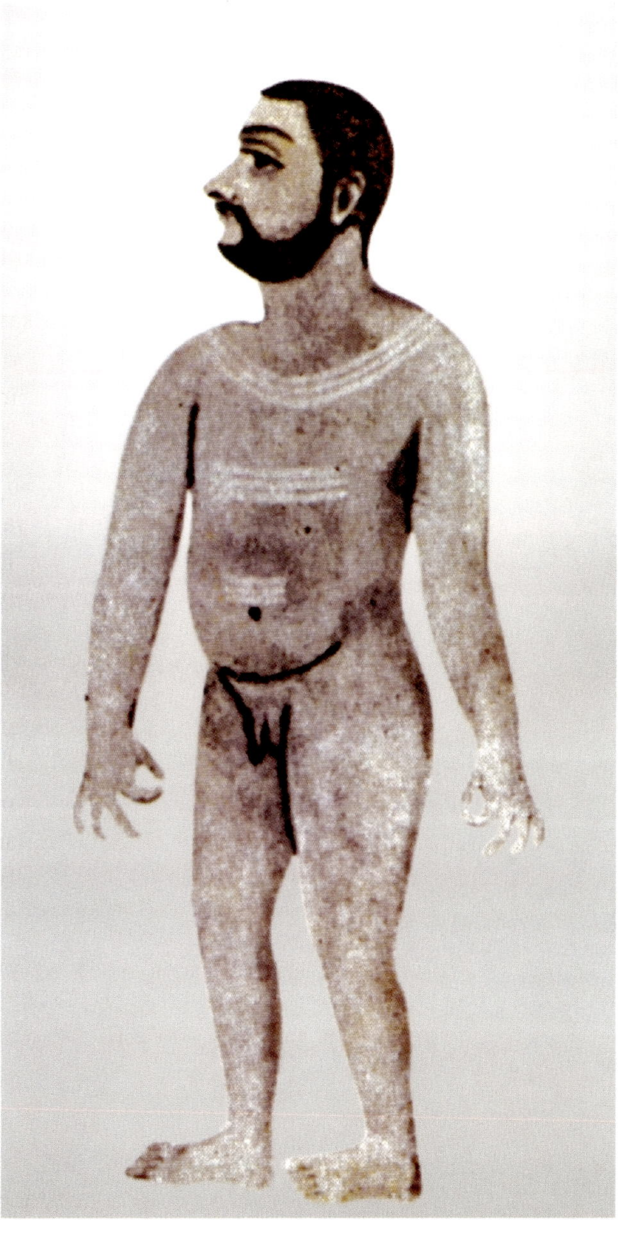

2. Sadashiva Brahmendrar.

depth of his knowledge of the Shastras, Vedas, and Upanishads. He never spent time playing with other boys, but was whole-heartedly immersed in his studies.

At the proper age, the function of *chowlam* (shaving the head in front and letting the hair grow behind to be made into a tuft) was performed. Then his father as his first *guru* initiated him with the Gayatri *mantra* by the ritual known as *upanayana samskara*, and he attained the status of a *brahmachari*. As was the custom in those days, his marriage was also solemnized at a young age; the bride was a mere child.

But all these did not affect his studies, which he pursued with steadfastness. For him, all these were duties which he had to perform. But at this time, something occurred, which in a split moment changed the whole course of life for Sivaramakrishnan and he became the epitome of renunciation — the *avadhuta* saint Sadashiva Brahmendrar. One day, a messenger from Sivaramakrishnan's wife's house came to Somanatha Avadhanigal's house and conveyed the happy news that their daughter-in-law had attained puberty. Sivaramakrishnan's mother was overjoyed, as it would mean that the girl would now soon come to her husband's house. Parvati was eagerly waiting for this event, as once her daughter-in-law came home, the burden of her house-work would be shared by her. She got busy and bustled about making arrangements to invite the *sambhandi*s (son's "parents-in-law") for a grand feast.

Sivaramakrishnan who had gone for his study returned home for his midday meal. He was usually very hungry when he came home for his lunch and would get angry if he was not served at once. When he told his mother to serve his food, she excitedly told him "Pichu, your wife has attained puberty; I have invited your in-laws for a feast, so please wait." There was nothing wrong in this statement, but for a person absorbed in spirituality, these words of his mother broke the slender thread by which he was attached to worldly life. His mind made a rapid calculation "when I was married, I was too young to realize the implications of it — wife, children, earning for the family and being bound to this *samsara sagara* for life. In this first step, I have to forego my meals. If I allow these bonds to strengthen, it will be difficult to break away. It is better not to enter a cave, rather than enter it, and then flounder about in the dark." Sivaramakrishnan was hungry and did not get his midday meal. The reason for this sparked off a thought process which ended in a hunger for spiritual knowledge. His mother's words were the initiation for his renunciation.

One cannot however come to the conclusion that spiritual knowledge will lead to renunciation. There were two scholars who studied with Sivaramakrishnan in the *gurukula*. One was Sridhara Ayyaval; the other was Mahabhashyam Gopalakrishna Shastrigal. Both of them chose to tread different paths which however was not the path of celibacy and renunciation. Shridhara Ayyaval lived the life of a householder, but without any attachment and became a saint; Gopalakrishna Shastri followed the *Guru-parampara* and taught scholars. Sri Ramakrishna Paramahamsa had no education whatsoever, he did not study the Vedas or the Shastras, but he had God realization, and had eminent degree holders sitting at his feet and listening to him.

Renouncing family and all material possessions, Sadashiva rushed to the feet of his *guru* and surrendered himself to him. He regarded his *guru* as his God and served him devotedly. Guru Paramasivendrar taught his favourite student all that he knew. Sadashiva was quick to grasp whatever was taught so that very soon he excelled his *guru*. His knowledge of the Shastras was profound.

Since Paramashivendrar was a renowned teacher, scholars came from far-off places to learn from him and take part in the *vidvat sabhas* or assemblage of scholars whose lengthy discussions were based on Tarka Shastra that is the science of logic. This meant analysing the Vedas and Shastras in discussions and arguments. Sadashiva revelled in these discussions. He would argue with the learned scholars and tear threadbare the theories and conclusions built-up by them. Sadashiva's knowledge was so vast and profound and he was so eloquent that many a time his opponent would feel humiliated. That was not Sadashiva's intention, nor was he arrogant, but it was his scholarliness that enabled him to defeat anyone by his convincing arguments.

Once during such a session when Sadashiva was arguing vehemently his *guru* lost his temper and in anger said, "Sadashiva, will you never shut your mouth?" As soon as he heard these words from his *guru*, he said "I will do so at once *gurudeva*, with your blessings," and Sadashiva shut his mouth and never spoke a word after that all his life. To be articulate and not to speak is a *sadhana* which only a saint of Sadashiva Brahmendrar's calibre can achieve.

Wearing the ochre robe does not make a man a *sannyasi*, if the mind hankers after material things. Sadashiva Brahmendrar found it irksome even to wear clothes, as one would have to wash them, keep them clean, and get new ones when the old ones were worn out. So he decided to dispense with the wearing of clothes to cover his body. Gradually, even the *kaupinam* or loin-cloth slipped away and he became an *avadhuta* or naked saint. Seeing him wandering naked, some recognized his greatness and worshipped him and gave him food, but many were those who mocked at him and abused him.

The vagaries of nature, the sun's heat, cold, rain, nothing affected him. But even an *avadhuta* would require food for sustenance, wouldn't he? But for Sadashiva Brahmendrar who had renounced speech, clothes and comfort was it difficult to conquer hunger? He therefore controlled his tongue, subsisting on almost anything — green leaves, dry leaves, berries, whatever he found — a little would suffice.

Sadashiva did not stay at one place, but roamed forests and went into deep spells of samadhi for hours, oblivious to the world.

Power and *siddhi*s came to him naturally and the *ashtamadhi siddhi* (eight kinds of spiritual powers) surrendered to him. But he never cared for the power which the *siddhi*s gave him. Once when a devotee told Bhagavan Ramana Maharishi, "Bhagavan, we believe that when we pray to you, miracles have happened, so how do you say you do not perform miracles?" Bhagavan smiled and said it is not his will that makes miracles happen but each time it is a divine automatic action which appears as a miracle.

There is an interesting episode in the life of Ramakrishna Paramahamsa. Once the Master offered to give the power of the *siddhi*s to Vivekananda. The latter asked him "Master, will this help me in my spiritual quest?" "No," replied the Master. "In a way they may be a hindrance, but by this you can attain name, fame and wealth." Vivekananda replied, "then keep the *siddhi*s for yourself."

Sadashiva Brahmendrar was a siddhar. He never cared for such powers, but he has used them on occasions when he wanted to. Swamigal lost all worldly consciousness and he lived in a state of bliss neither knowing what he was doing, nor where he was going. Many times his trance-like state landed him in trouble but nothing seemed to touch his conscience.

Once, he was roaming along a river bank at a place called Kodimudi, and suddenly sat down on a pile of sand, and went into deep meditation. In the evening, the tide came and brought with it more sand. Sadashiva Bramendrar was buried, sitting, by a huge mound of sand. It started raining. Eventually the rain stopped and gradually the sand mound grew bigger. The rainy season was over and summer followed. The farmers came with implements to dig sluices in order to make the river water flow to the fields. While digging, one of the men found blood on his shovel. The men who gathered there were frightened as to what they might discover when they removed the huge sand pile. They carefully removed the sand and saw buried deep in the pit, a naked man in a state of meditation. "O! What is this? This is some holy *mahatma*," they exclaimed in wonder and awe. Sadashiva Brahmendrar opened his eyes on hearing the sounds of shouting, and getting up, dusted the sand off himself and walked away unconcerned about the blood flowing from his shoulder. The men stood stupefied at this strange sight.

For saints who have acquired *animadhi* (eight kinds of spiritual powers also referred to as *ashtamadhi siddhi*s) *siddhi*, there is no miracle they cannot perform, but they never think much of *siddhi*s and never bother to exhibit them. But once in a while, in a playful mood they have manifested miracles. So it happened when Sadashiva Brahmendrar was roaming the green woods of Karur. Very often children from the village would bring sweetmeats or other eatables for their *thatha* (grandfather). One day, the children were playing there, and surrounded him and said — all of them shouting at the same time — "*Thatha, thatha*, please take us to Madurai, there is a festival going on there, please, *thatha,*" they clamoured. The saint gestured to all of them to climb on to him. Some hung on his arms, some on his shoulders; some clung around his neck and his head. He gestured to them to close their eyes, and when he gave the signal to open their eyes, they were in Madurai. It was indeed a festival day. The main deities Meenakshi and her consort Sundaresvarar, were being taken round in a procession. The children were delighted to see the temple. The procession of the deities was carried on a chariot drawn by men; and the chariot accompanied by music, dancing and singing, went round the temple streets. The divine *thatha* also provided them with plenty of goodies to eat. The children were now tired and wanted to go home. The mode of transport was the same. They closed their eyes, and when they opened them they were back in Karur. The children ran home happy and excited, and told their parents of their trip to Madurai, proof of which was the packet of sweets they had brought home. Needless to say, the whole of Karur was stunned by this miracle and felt blessed to have such a saint in their midst.

But Sadashiva Brahmendrar moved on from Karur, and in another place, another miracle happened. It was harvest time, and the harvested stocks of grains were heaped like pyramids. As Sadashiva Brahmendrar's passage was blocked by just such a grain heap, he leant against it and went to sleep in that posture. Some men who came there thought it was a thief who had come to steal the grain, and they lifted their hands to give him some hard blows but the hands they lifted remained lifted and they could not bring them down. They remained in agony in that position throughout the night. In the morning, when the owner came to inspect the grain, he found his men moaning in pain. He fell at the feet of the saint and begged his forgiveness. Sadashiva woke up and quietly walked away and the men could now bring down their hands.

On another occasion, in a village, the Munsif was arranging a grand feast for a visiting dignitary. The whole village was engaged in this work. Some people were sent to fetch vegetables and fruits, some for bringing provisions, and some men were sent to cut wood from the forest as fuel for cooking. As there was a lot of wood to be carried, someone spotted the *avadhuta* saint and assuming him to be a tribal, they put a load of firewood on his head. He quietly walked along with the others carrying loads of wood. When they got to the place where the wood was to be deposited, Sadashiva Brahmendrar also unloaded his load on to the heaped wood and lo! the whole wood pile burst into flames, appearing as if there was a huge bonfire. The village officials and the men realized that they had asked a great saint to carry firewood, and falling at his feet begged for forgiveness. Sadashiva Brahmendrar, with a beatific smile, blessed all of them and walked away casually.

During important festival days such as *Janmashtami*, *Sivaratri*, etc. he would be seen in several shrines simultaneously. Those fortunate ones who were there could see the miracle of the saint standing outside the *garbha-griha*, performing *archana*, and reciting the *mantra*s. Simultaneously, in the *garbha-griha*, beautiful fragrant flowers fell one by one on the deity, as he recited the *mantra*s from outside.

Once an illiterate, ignorant *brahmachari* kept on following the Swamigal wherever he went, wanting his blessings. Sadashiva Brahmendrar was full of compassion. He understood the yearning of the young man and blessed him. One day, the brahmin expressed a wish to the saint that he wanted to have darshan of Sri Ranganatha in Srirangam. The saint gestured to him to close his eyes, and the next minute both of them were standing in front of the reclining Ranganatha Swamy. When the *brahmachari* opened his eyes after meditation and prayer, his *guru* was not there. The *brahmachari* was inconsolable with grief. He looked for his *guru* everywhere. At last, Sadashiva Brahmendrar took pity on him and appeared before him. With love and compassion for this devotee, he initiated him with a *mantra*, writing it on the sand, and also in writing, advised him to accept Gopalakrishna Shastri as his *guru*. Because of his *guru*'s grace, the illiterate *brahmachari* acquired learning and knowledge and became an exponent of the Puranas, and conducted discourses. He became famous and was known as Akasha Purana Ramalinga Sastrigal.

In another incident, as the sage was wandering aimlessly without being aware of himself, he walked into the garden of the harem of a Muslim *zamindar*. When the *zamindar* saw a naked man going into the women's quarters, he was furious, and taking a huge knife, ran in pursuit of the saint who was walking in a state of bliss. The *zamindar* caught hold of the saint, and with his knife chopped off his right hand from the elbow. The hand fell lifeless on the ground, and his blood drenched the street. Still Sadashiva Brahmendrar kept walking, aware neither of blood flowing, nor feeling pain. The *zamindar* realised that this was no ordinary man, but a great saint. He picked up the fallen hand and ran behind the sage, and when he reached him, he fell at his feet and begged for forgiveness. Sadashiva Brahmendrar looked at the severed hand and at his stump of an arm. He just fitted the hand into the socket, and it became whole again without a trace of the injury and walked on. The *zamindar* fell at his feet and begged of the saint to give him some advice which he could treasure and follow till the end of his life. The saint, struck by his earnestness, wrote on the dust of the street "Do not do what you want, then you may do what you like." After the saint left, the *zamindar* wanted to return home, but the advice of the saint prevented him. He wanted to walk to ease his limbs, but remembering the *guru*'s advice, he could not. He was hungry and wanted to eat, but said "no" to himself. He practized this denial of what he wanted, and one day, suddenly realised that he was free from the burdens imposed by his body and mind and that he was in control of his senses. Caste and religion had nothing to teach him, and he gradually attained spiritual bliss.

It is said that Sadashiva Brahmendrar had his *samadhi* at three places — Karachi, Nerur, and Manamadurai.

When the saint wandered through the forests in Puducottah, the Raja of Puducottah, Vijaya Raghunath Thondaiman used to meet him there. He was a great devotee of the saint. Sadashiva also knew the *raja* to be pure-hearted and a true devotee, and he initiated him into a mantra. Since the saint did not speak, he wrote the *mantra* on the sand. The raja read the *mantra* and memorized it. The sand on which the *mantra* was written was carefully gathered in a silver casket and placed in the palace *puja* room for daily worship, and, during the *Navaratri* festival, special prayers were offered.

The *avadhuta* saint, Sadashiva Brahmendrar, who had been a constant wanderer, suddenly felt tired of his life, and decided to hasten his eternal *samadhi*.

The *maharaja* of Tanjore, Saraboji, became an ardent devotee of the saint. *Sadashiva*'s blessing and inspiration was responsible for the *maharaja*'s founding of the famous Saraswati Mahal Library at Tanjore.

Even though Sadashiva Brahmendrar had roamed the length and breadth of Tamil Nadu, his heart was at the banks of the river Kaveri. He chose his own time and place for his last resting place. Kaveri flowed throughout Tamil territory (and also in Karnataka where it is called Talakkaveri). On the banks of this river was the town of Nerur, the place chosen by the saint for his ultimate *samadhi*. He settled in Nerur, and made his abode among the trees and flowers in the woods. Everyone was surprised that this nomadic saint had settled down in one place. The people of Nerur served him with great devotion, and were grateful for the opportunity.

One day, he was seen in the Nerur *agraharam* (brahmin village). Some devotees came to pay their obeisance to him. To them, he gave a date and made signs that on that day, he would leave his earthly body. He also indicated that on that day, someone will be coming from Kashi with a *Banalingam*, and that this *lingam* should be installed beside his *samadhi*. The brahmin devotees who were given these instructions piously waited for that holy day, when this great event was to take place.

The day appointed by the saint dawned. On the shores of the river Kaveri, where the sand was thickest, a huge pit, long and deep was dug in accordance with the saint's instructions. All the necessary articles for the rituals were collected. A huge crowd from far and near had assembled there. *Pundit*s were loudly chanting Vedic *mantra*s. People were watching with bated breadth. Everyone was waiting to have a glimpse of the great saint, before he went into eternal rest. They stood with folded hands, tears streaming down their faces.

At the exact time he had appointed, Avadhuta Swamigal Shri Sadashiva Brahmendrar came, and with a divine smile on his face, calmly walked to the *samadhi* pit. There were shouts of "Jaya Jaya! Sadashiva Brahmendrar Swamigal, Jaya Jaya!" Tears flowed freely from everybody's eyes. Swamigal looked at the vast crowd of people, and with his eyes, blessed them all. At once, without any hesitation, he went into the *samadhi* pit. He indicated by a gesture that now all the rituals could begin. According to the Shastras, the last rites accorded to a saint were done. According to Hindu scriptures, there was no ritual cremation for one who had voluntarily given up his soul. The pit was sealed.

Till late that night, the chanting of *mantra*s went on. At last, everything was still, the crowds dispersed. Then, now and forever, the beacon that was Sadashiva Brahmendrar the mouni, the *avadhuta*, the saint composer, shines from the open space, which he loved.

Hearing of the nirvana of the Swamigal, Vijaya Raghunatha Raja of Puducottah came post-haste and undertook the expenses of the remaining rituals, which went on for ten days. The brahmin from Kashi, arrived with the *Banalinga*, which was installed beside his *samadhi*. Raja Vijaya Raghunatha built a temple over the *samadhi*. All expenses of maintenance and the daily *puja* were undertaken by the Puducottai state. In the year 1912, a *sannyasi* came there and started the *paddhati* (practice) of *laksharchana* (the performance of worship with flowers along with the recitation of the name of God one lakh times) every year. This practice continues till date. Shri Sadashiva Brahmendrar had composed and sung many songs and written commentaries. His musical compositions are sung or played on instruments at the end of almost every major carnatic music concert. It can be truly said that Sadashiva Brahmendrar was one of the greatest sages of the eighteenth century.

8

Avudai Akkal

THE eighteenth century has produced a plethora of saints. Among them a woman saint named Avudai Akkal stands out for her poetic genius. Her life is intertwined with that of her *guru* Sridhara Venkatesa Ayyaval who accepted the child widow Avudai as his disciple and showed her the path to salvation. There has been no record anywhere of her life. Whatever facts have come to light are mainly from her own compositions painstakingly pieced together by Srimathi Gomathi Rajangam and Ayakudi Venkatarama Sastri from the people of Shencottah, the birthplace of Avudai Akkal. Facts about her life have been passed on from generation to generation by word of mouth and through her songs, which are sung by Tamil brahmin women on every festive occasion. It took years of research and effort to collect handwritten manuscripts, which were family treasures and get them published. The most comprehensive account of her works to date is by Svami Satchidananda Svamigal of Tirukkoyil in North Arcot district.

Two hundred fifty years ago, a girl was born into an orthodox brahmin family. She was named Avudai after the Goddess Avudai (one of the names of Parvati). She grew up to be a charming, intelligent child. Her parents and grandparents adored her. As was the custom then, she was married at a very young age. It was said that before the bridal flowers could fade, she became a widow. There was wailing

3. Avudai Akkal.

and weeping by the elders and relatives in the house. Seeing this, the child Avudai asked her mother, "Amma, why are you all crying?" Hearing her reply that she was crying for the death of the bridegroom, Avudai said, "why are you crying for somebody else's son?"

At once her mother asked everyone to stop weeping. Yes, what the child says is true, why should we weep for someone else's son? We elders do not have the wisdom of this little girl, she thought, and gathered her little daughter in her arms. From that day she dressed up the child in fine clothes and decked her with jewels. Her mother also asked some *pundit*s to teach her daughter. But in this effort, the village people, who opposed the girl being given any learning, thwarted her. Of what use is learning to a girl who is a widow and would have to spend all her life in the kitchen not showing her face outside that domain, they argued vehemently. Regarding her wearing silk and jewellery they were simply shocked and scolded and abused Avudai's mother for this defiance of the brahmin society. But her mother stood firm in her resolve to see her little girl have some happiness before she underwent the punishment meted out to widows even if they were little children.

The fateful day came when Avudai attained puberty. For three days, she was confined in a room. On the fourth day, after the ritual bath the mother saw her daughter's long hair, which she had lovingly combed and decorated with flowers, shaved. She was then given a nine-yard white sari to wear. Avudai lay in a corner of a room stunned by what had happened to her. It took many days for the girl to realize the enormity of her plight. She wept and wept and prayed to God, if there was one, to save her, to take her out of this hell and give her enlightenment.

Sridhara Venkatesa Ayyaval, a famous saint who lived by *unjhavritti,* an ancient practice of subsisting by singing devotional songs in front of the homes and thus collecting alms, was coming to the village of Shencottah where Avudai lived. Normally prior notice is given to the people before any great person visits so that they could make preparations to receive him with due honour. But Ayyaval did not give any such prior information. Even so, the villagers came to know of his visit and were busy making prepartions. The women of the brahmin *agraharam* (meaning brahmin settlement) got up at three in the morning and sprinkled water mixed with cow dung in front of their house and made elaborate patterns of *kolam* or *rangoli* with rice powder and coloured powder. In each house, the men had an early bath and were waiting near the entrance to the village with the *purna kumbam* — a decorated brass pitcher of water — with mango leaves and a coconut in the centre, this being the traditional way of welcoming a distinguished guest. The streets were lined with children and women holding plates of flower petals to be strewn on the path Ayyaval would walk. It was well past morning and still no sign of the great saint. In each house the women and men were waiting with water to wash the feet of the saint and offer him fruits and coconut, concluding their worship with the performance of a*rati*. At last they heard the sound of the anklets Ayyaval wore on his feet as he danced, singing prayers of the Lord. The whole village was decorated with festoons and flowers, but one house in Attangkarai Street was silent. There was no light in the house, no neat frontage decorated with *kolam*s, and the door was closed.

Sridhara Venkatesa Ayyaval walked through the *agraharam* receiving the welcome offered by the householders and came to Attangkarai Street and stood in front of the house whose doors were closed and the sound of weeping could be heard.

He stood there singing *bhajans* like *Govinda Hare Mukunda* and dancing. He also kept strumming his *tambura* (stringed instrument) which hung on his chest. He went on singing till suddenly the door was flung open and the figure of a young woman came running out and fell at the feet of the saint. Her head was tonsured and was covered by the end of her white cotton *sari*. She held his feet and wept her heart out. Ayyaval gently raised her and placing his hand on her head blessed her, and said, "My child, do not weep. God is with you. Come and see me in the evening near the river." By this time people from the house came and took her inside. The young woman was Avudai.

The brahmins of the village who were a witness to all this, suddenly lost interest in Ayyaval and made snide remarks about a saint touching and lifting a woman. What kind of a saint was this, they said. In the remaining houses of the village there was no welcome for Ayyaval. Ayyaval walked without a glance at the villagers and went to the stone structure — *mandapam* — on the banks of the river.

Avudai's family guarded her to prevent her from going to the river bank in the evening to meet Ayyaval. Already the village was buzzing with scandalous gossip. If Avudai went to meet Ayyaval, the family would be ostracized from the village. But Avudai was firm in her resolve to go to meet the saint. Her mother's advice to her fell on deaf ears. Since everyone had to go out, some on work, some on the daily temple visit, they left a woman to keep guard over her, and went out. Avudai by cajoling the woman with tearful entreaties, asked her to come with her to the river as a chaperon so that no blame would fall on her.

Avudai reached the river bank just as the sun was setting, and it was getting dark. Avudai with her heart pounding stood in a corner of the *mandapam*. For a momment she felt dizzy, next minute she saw the saintly figure of Ayyaval standing before her, with *vibhuti* drawn in three lines across his forehead, a *rudrakshamala* around his neck, he appeared like Lord Shiva himself to her.

Avudai fell at his feet. Ayyaval stroked her head, helped her to get up by lending support with his hands and made her sit. "My child, open your eyes, look at me and accept me as your *guru*. From today the doors of spiritual knowledge will be opened to you. I will initiate you with a *mantra* which you must keep repeating without fear. Whatever the world or society might say, do not heed them or be hurt by them. I will always guide you and see to your progress on the spiritual path." So saying, he blessed her and disappeared into the darkness of the night.

What initiation Avudai got from her *guru*, and how she progressed in her *sadhana* are all written in her songs "Advaita Aandi" and "Pandithan Kavi." She was lost in meditation and remained in the state of *samadhi* (spiritual trance) for hours. The orthodox brahmins of the village decided to excommunicate her and banish her from the village. Under her *guru*'s guidance, Avudai left her village and went on a pilgrimage.

She visited many temples and had many spiritual visions and experiences. For several hours everyday she would repeat the *mantra* her *guru* had given her and sit in meditation. Whenever she needed help or guidance her guru would guide her.

There have been many incidents of miracles and extraordinary events during the journey on foot by Avudai Akkal (*akkal* = elder sister) to various places, but unfortunately there is no record of her pilgrimages. No chronicler wrote them down. The only record is what she has herself written in her songs, many of which are lost to us.

One incident which is known is about her visit to Ramanathapuram where she was given a grand welcome and honoured by the *raja* of Ramnad. It is said that the *raja* had sent 108 gold coins to Avudai Akkal for performing *archana* to *Shivalinga* during her *puja*. His purpose may have been to test her reputation for complete renunciation of material things including gold. Avudai Akkal in her evening *puja* along with flowers offered one by one the 108 gold coins. The next morning Akkal collected all the previous day's flowers along with the gold coins and threw them in the river. When the *raja* came to know about this he was amazed, he realized that gold or flowers made no difference to a saint like Avudai Akkal.

Another incident that is known about her spiritual travels, is that once Avudai Akkal blocked the path of the Shankaracharya Sri "Ugra" Narasimha Bharati Swamigal, the Pontiff of the Sringeri Mutt, an institution that subscribed to the traditional belief that its Pontiffs should not even look at widows. She told the Acharya:

> I have in me the tune and the song,
> but no space to air it

The Acharya Ugra Narasimha Bharati is purported to have responded to her in the same poetic vein:

> Can a fast spreading creeper
> ever be arrested?
> Spread.

Avudai Akkal's 65 stanza poem called *Jnana Ammanai* is dedicated to Acharya Ugra Narasimha Bharati. Rejecting the "Ugra" (fiery) she addresses him as "Shanta Narasimha."

After her long pilgrimage to many sacred places Avudai Akkal came to Mayavaram in Tanjavur district. Akkal went to the river Kaveri to bathe and while she was bathing she saw a mango leaf come floating towards her. It looked as if it was chewed and thrown by someone. But Akkal, who had already progressed so much in the spiritual path had no inhibitions. She took the leaf out of the water and cleaned her teeth with it. It must be said here that in those days people brushed their teeth with the twig of a *neem* or *peepal* tree or with a mango leaf before bathing and threw it in the river. So it is to be taken that Avudai Akkal knew it was an *ecchil* (meaning one polluted by human saliva) leaf and whose it was. The other women who were bathing there abused her for using a leaf used by someone else, but Akkal did not mind their abuse. She only smiled and after finishing her bath as she came up the steps she saw her Guru Sri Ayyaval sitting under a spreading banyan tree. She went and prostrated before him. Ayyaval wrote the *Bijakshara mantra OM* on her tongue and blessed her. He then told her, "you have now attained the state of a *Jivana Mukta*. You are freed from *karma* and will have no more births and deaths. Now you can go back to your birthplace Shencottah and live there."

By this time the greatness of Akkal had reached her village. Sri Avudai Akkal's songs steeped in Advaita attracted many disciples, who followed her to Shencottah. The widow whom they had humiliated and banished was now their pride. The people of her village now welcomed her as a celebrity. Avudai lived for many years in Shencottah spreading the message of Advaita through her songs to those devotees who flocked from far and near to see her.

Years passed. One *amavasya* day in the month of Adi (corresponding to July middle to August middle) Avudai

Akkal went to the nearby waterfall in Kuttralam, with many devotees following her. After a bath in the waterfall she climbed the mountain alone, saying she wanted to meditate for some time, and was never seen again. Even after a thorough search her body was never found. Her disappearance remains a mystery to this day.

The poetical genius of Avudai Akkal was enshrined in more than 1,000 compositions of which barely one tenth have survived. It was the practise in most of the surrounding villages in and around Shencottah for women to get together and sing Akkal's songs. After the passing away of her *guru* who actually merged with the Lord in the Mahalinga Temple in Tiruvidaimaruthur, Avudai Akkal composed the *Anubhava Ratnamala* in a lamenting tune called *Pilakkanam* sung as dirges for the dead. Akkal's *Pilakkanam* extolled the greatness of her Guru Sridhara Venkateswara Ayyaval.

Her other important composition was "Chudalai Kummi" which is from the famous Sanskrit text *Jnana Vasishtham.* It seems Akkal had written other stories from the *Jnana Vasishtham*, but they are not available. She has composed the entire *Bhagavad Gita* in verse in Tamil. Also of note is the *Vidhai Shobhanam* which is in the frolicsome mood of a song sung by friends when a girl attains puberty, which is more or less advice to a maiden on the threshold of becoming a wife and mother. Akkal's *Shobhanam* is different in that the maturity that is spoken of here is not a biological or physical one but a spiritual one and the ultimate union is not between man and woman but the individual soul and the Supreme Soul.

The Ammanai composition dedicated to the Pontiff of Sringeri Ugra Narasimha Bharati is a game played by girls. Shining coloured balls, three or four, are tossed up and caught without dropping any single ball — this also has a philosophical connotation. The game in its metaphysical underpinnings means that even while performing your household duties your goal should be a one-pointed concentration on the spiritual fountainhead.

The life of this saint who was a child widow of seven years and evolved as one of the greatest women saints of the eighteenth century is an amazing one. Unfortunately no scholar has taken up this as a research project — perhaps with persistence and perseverance more facts about her life may emerge.

Part III

Saints of Modern Period

9

Sri Kuzhanthaiyanandar Swamigal

MADURAI a city in south India was famous for many reasons. It was ruled by a woman, the goddess Parvati as Queen Meenakshi, and not by a king. Her consort was Lord Sundareswar. Meenakshi was Parvati and Sundareswar was Shiva who had manifested on earth as the daughter of the King Malayadvaja Pandyan, and her divine consort. Madurai was the seat of the third Tamil Sangam, where poets congregated and had their works approved by the *Sangampalakai* (Sangam plank).

Later the temple built for Goddess Meenakshi and Sundareswar was one of the most exquisite architectural wonders of south India. The whole city lay around the temple. It was built by King Tirumala Nayakar. In the most sacred temple city was born a saint who was an extraordinary child brought up by Goddess Meenakshi herself.

Sri Ramaswamy Iyer of Madurai was a well-to-do man and his wife's name was Tripurasundari. They were a pious couple. They would visit the Meenakshi temple and worship Devi with great devotion everyday. They undertook the expense of the special poojas conducted in the temple. In those days the rituals of worship and the expenses were borne by the devotees themselves. The temple administration was under a Trust formed by the village elders. The temple *archaka*s brought the food offerings for the gods and goddesses from their homes. The temple was managed from the generosity of the donors.

4. Sri Kuzhandaiyananda Svamigal.

Sri Ramaswamy Iyer and his wife Tripurasundari were childless. They prayed intensely to Devi Meenakshi to bless them with a child. Tripurasundari herself made the sweet rice *Pongal* and other delicacies for offering as *prasada* to Meenakshi Ambal. Her husband would carry a basket of fruits, betel leaves and nuts, and flower garlands for the special *puja*s performed on festival days. One day as they went to the temple carrying all these items for the special *puja,* Ramaswamy Iyer walked ahead and entered the temple. When his wife came to the main *gopura* entrance two beggar children approached her and in a supplicating manner said, "Amma, Amma, we are very hungry, give us some of the sweetmeats you are carrying." They went behind her, begging her to give something to eat. The lady said, "Please wait for some time, I am taking these for Ambal and after the *naivedyam* (offering) is done, when I return I will give you lots of *prasada* to eat." But the two beggar boys looked so pitifully at her with tears in their eyes that Tripurasundari's motherly instincts were aroused and seeing the tears flowing from the cheeks of those innocent children her heart melted, and she gave away all that she had brought and taking only the fruit basket her husband had handed over to her, went into the temple.

Ramaswamy Iyer was impatiently waiting for his wife to give the *prasada* to the *archakar* when she came and told him that she had given away the *prasada* offerings to two beggar boys. He became livid with anger and disappointment. He felt it was an ill omen that they could not give the *prasada* for Meenakshi Ambal. As he did not feel like staying for the *abhishekam* and other rituals he went home in a huff. Tripurasundari stood in front of Devi and prayed for a long time, and came home to face her husband in trepidation and fear. As she expected her husband was sitting in an angry mood in the *payol* and near him a boy was standing with a plate. "Amma, you forgot to take the *prasadam* with you, Ayyaval here says this is not your *prasada* as you did not bring any today. What can I do? This is your *prasada*, please take it Amma," he pleaded.

Tripurasundari took the plate from the boy and was amazed to find it was the same sweet preparations and *vadai* she had given the beggar boys and the quantity was the same.

Tripurasundari knew it was Meenakshi Ambal's grace and blessing and the two beggar boys were her messengers. Overwhelmed with tears streaming from her eyes she reverently touched the food to her eyes, and looked at her husband. By this time the boy had left. Tripurasundari urged her husband to follow the boy and find out who he was. He at once went behind the boy, but when he reached the *gopuram* entrance the boy disappeared. That was where the two beggar boys got the *prasada* items.

Ramaswamy Iyer realized now that it was Ambal's *lila*. He returned home and told his wife that the boy had disappeared at the gateway of the temple and this was a miracle he had himself witnessed. It was Meenakshi Ambal's blessings for them. With great emotion they went over the events and rejoiced at the divine grace of the Goddess which had been showered on them in abundance.

Ten months after this miracle took place Tripurasundari gave birth to twin boys. They were named Rama and Lakshmana, and the proud parents took great care of them. There was no difference at least in appearance between the two boys. However, there was one striking difference. Rama never suckled milk from his mother's breast but a milky saliva flowed from the corners of the infant's mouth. The parents thought that there was something wrong with the child. Tripurasundari when she had prayed for a child had taken a vow that if Goddess Meenakshi made her a mother and removed the stigma of being a barren woman, she would give her first born to Meenakshi Ambal and leave the child in the temple. She knew that she made this vow, but the mother's heart filled with love for her twin boys made her forget it. But the divine mother did not forget the promise made by Tripurasundari. She appeared in her dream and asked her to give one child to her as per her vow.

Ramaswamy Iyer when he heard of his wife's dream decided to immediately take the baby to the temple and leave it in the custody of Goddess Meenakshi. But which one should they give? They were in a dilemma. One day the couple with the twins went to the temple for worship. The *archakar* suddenly as if possessed said loudly "whichever child has the mark of a conch and *chakra* on the soles of his feet should be left here." The parents put both the infants down before the Goddess. Rama went crawling on all fours lisping, "Amma, Amma" towards the idol of Devi. The *archakar* lifted the child and examined his feet. He found the mark of the conch and the *chakra* on the soles of the infant's feet. Everyone recognized that it was a divine child, and touched the child's feet with both hands and put their hands to their eyes in reverence. The parents placed the baby Rama at the feet of the Goddess Meenakshi and went home with the other twin Lakshmana.

The last *puja* of the night was over and the *archakar* was about to shut the doors of the temple, when he suddenly remembered that a little child was there. He thought, "What can I do with this child, where can I leave him?"

From the *garbha-griha* he heard a voice "let the child be here." The *archakar* knew it was Ambal's command and left the child with Ambal and locked the *garbha-griha* and went home.

The little child Rama grew up in the temple. The *archakar*s fed him with milk and mashed rice, devotees bathed him, and he played in the temple happily, the favourite of one and all. They called him Rajagopalan. As he grew up the *archakar*s performed his *upanayanam* (thread ceremony). They decided to send him to Kashi to study under the eminent Sanskrit Pundit Ganapathy Baba. Strangely Ganapathy Baba himself came to Madurai to worship Devi Meenakshi. The temple *archakar*s entrusted the boy to him and Rama, called Rajagopalan by the devotees, went to Kashi with Ganapathy Baba.

At this time Sri Ramaswamy Iyer passed away, having completed his *karma* on this earth. His wife who was devoted to him entered the funeral pyre of her husband and became a *sati*. The other twin Lakshmana was taken care of by the relatives of the deceased couple. It is recorded that in that family every year *Sumangali Puja* is performed in her memory.

The proof that Tripurasundari, the mother of the child Rama, was herself imbued with divinity was that on the next day of her committing *sati* a man named Chokkalinganadar was passing through the cremation grounds and found ear-rings, bangles, the pleated part of a silk *sari* and a fresh lime fruit. He was amazed and picked these articles and took them home. That night Tripurasundari came in his dream and wanted him to keep these articles in a pot[1] and perform *puja* for it. Accordingly for generations that sacred pot has been a family possession and the first girl child was called Papathi Amma (brahmin girl) in her memory. It is interesting that Tripurasundari should have manifested herself to someone

1. It is customary among some Tamil families to revere and worship any woman in the family who had died as a *sumangali* (that is while her husband still lived). Annually a saree with her auspicious articles, such as turmeric and bangles, is kept in an earthen pot and worshipped. The pot is *called poovadai paanai.*

who was a non-brahmin.

Sri Kuzhanthaiyanandar the child Rajagopalan's new name — was initiated into the Srividya *mantra* by Goddess Meenakshi herself. But following the normal practice of studying in the *gurukula* of a *guru* his divine mother chose Ganapathy Baba — who bore the name of her first son Ganapathy — to instruct the boy in the study of Sanskrit, the Vedas and the Upanishads. It is said that Ganapathy Baba was ageless, his age could be 90 or 900. In Kashi he was known as Ganapathy Brahman. The *samadhi* of this great *guru* can be seen in the Panchalinga building in Kashi. There is also a marble statue of him erected over the *samadhi*.

Kuzhanthaiyanandar learnt at the feet of this great *guru* everything there was to be learnt and mastered, not only all the Shastras and Vedas, but all the *siddhis*. He was initiated and given the name Trilinga Swami by his *guru*.

Trilinga Swami wandered in the Himalayas for many years as an *avadhudhar* (naked saint). It is said of Kuzhanthaiyanandar, now Trilinga Swami, that he lived for 100 years, and his first *samadhi* was in Kashi. In Kashi in the Panchalinga platform his *samadhi* can be seen near the *samadhi* of his Guru Ganapathy Brahman. Trilinga Swami arose from this *samadhi* and was seen roaming in several places after his physical death.

It was after he emerged again into the world after his *samadhi* at Kashi that he was sitting in the Pashupathinath Temple in Kathmandu, Nepal. While he was there he came to know that a member of the royal family was suffering from the dreaded disease — leprosy. The Swami miraculously cured him of the affliction. The royal family in gratitude presented him with a *makarakandi* and a *gourishankar rudrakshamala*. The Swami never removed these two *malas* from his neck. In pictures taken then of Trilinga Swami, he is wearing these *malas*. Thus one could infer that he went to Nepal as Trilinga Swami.

Sri Ramakrishna Paramahamsa and Sri Vivekananda have come to Kashi to have a *darshana* of Trilinga Swami. The story goes that the Swami was lying beneath a boat in the scorching sun when Paramahamsa came to see him, and had his *darshana* but could not speak to the Swami as he was observing silence — *mauna vrata*. But the Swami gestured by raising two fingers and then one, meaning that the *paramatma* and the *jivatma* although named separately were one, and Sri Ramakrishna understood it. It seems the Master said that of all the *yogi*s he had encountered in Kashi, Trilinga Swami was a true *brahmajnani*. Trilinga Swami had many disciples in the north. His second *samadhi* is said to be near the Pashupathinath Temple.

Next he was seen in south India, as if the need to enlighten the people of his region was his mission. The Swami himself declared that Trilinga Swami and Kuzhanthaiyanandar are one and the same.

Before his fourth *samadhi* when he was residing in Madurai in a house, he noticed that there was a picture of Trilinga Swami on the wall. Seeing this the Swami remarked, "Oho, here is a picture of me in this form! But here they have made me a child again and call me Kuzhanthaiyananda!" During his journey from the north to the south he had halted at many places and the *raja*s and *maharaja*s of those kingdoms had honoured him and worshipped him; the term *raja pujitha* was added to his *archana*.

The divine child of the divine mother Meenakshi did not need all these titles and praises, but for the people who benefited from his divine grace, how else could they show their devotion and gratitude? How else could they celebrate him? From there he went to Karnataka and Andhra bestowing blessings and dazzling people by miracles.

In Tiruvannamalai, he went into *samadhi* inside a pit which got covered with sand for several days. A devotee who had chosen this place to build a temple for Vinayakar (Ganapathy) while digging the ground for laying the foundation stone found blood pouring out, scaring everyone. The Swami got up from the pit and just walked away, unconcerned about the profuse bleeding from the cut.

The third *samadhi* was in Tenkasi, in Tirunelveli district, in the Sannidhi Madam Street. They say it is also the *samadhi* of Nellaiyappar, the deity in the Temple in Tirunelveli. The *samadhi* is in the house of one Shankar Pillai, a devotee of Swami. The Swami himself confirmed it. Once Kuzhanthiayanandar Swami collected 300 gold sovereigns for making a *srichakra meru*. He had come to his devotee Shankar Pillai's house to ask him to undertake the task of making it. He straightaway sat on the *samadhi*, which was in the house. The inmates did not approve of this. Whatever might be the greatness of this Swami they revered the Swami whose *samadhi* they worshipped in their home. The Swami understood their resentment and said "What! Have I to ask permission to sit on my own *samadhi*?" He said this and disappeared. He again then re-appeared on the site of the *samadhi* and blessed all of them.

How could all this happen? It seems unbelievable — but Swami Vivekananda himself has acknowledged the power of *siddhis* and accepts that saints can and do perform miracles.

As mentioned earlier, his fourth and final *samadhi* was in his own hometown of Madurai, but before that for more than 20 years, establishing himself in Madurai, he visited many places near about and blessed countless number of devotees. In the Tamil year of *Angirasa* in the month of *Purattasi* — corresponding to September on the 23rd a Saturday he went into eternal *samadhi*.

Although the Swami is not present in his physical form he performs miracles and responds to questions from devotees through the medium of a devotee chosen by him.

The life of Swami Kuzhanthiayanandar stands out among the lives of so many other saints because he was the beloved child of Sri Meenakshi Ambal. As Raja Rajeshwari, she sat on the transcendental throne of *sri chakra* and her beloved son could be no less. His birth was a miracle in itself, so his life is full of mysticism and miracles. He had all the powers of his Mother, so there is no need to be astonished or sceptical about his four *samadhi*s, his travels from the extreme south to extreme north in the Himalayas, Nepal and Kashi. Once he asked for some *kumkumam* (red vermillion powder sacred for Devi) when it was brought in a plate he threw small quantities of the red powder all over the room, and wonder of wonders, every bit of *kumkumam* became a *sri chakra*. Swami in exultation said "Look, look Devi has manifested, bring camphor and perform Arati for her!"

One L.V. Ramalingam Iyer a devotee of Sri Kuzhanthaiyanandar had the great fortune and blessing to be close to the Swami. He and his family served him devotedly and after his *samadhi* in Madurai they were entrusted with the *puja* and other rituals of the *samadhi*.

Once someone asked Swamigal "Swami, you have three dents on your back, what is the significance of that? He replied "Oh!, that, that is to say three are over, it is a sign." Maybe he meant the three *samadhi*s in Kashi, Nepal and Tenkasi.

Just before his final resting place or *samadhi* at Madurai, people noticed a divide between the three dents, and it swelled up into a ball. Those who saw it were frightened at the swelling, but the Swamigal was not in the least bothered. When he lay flat on his back the ball also became flat. Everyday it was the practice to massage Swamigal's body with melted ghee. The melted ghee when applied to his body hardened into solid ghee and no amount of heating and melting would prevent it from solidifying. For hours the devotees would take turns to massage his body. Then he would bathe in water heated by the sun's heat. Sometimes he would not bathe and just go away.

In 1932, Swamigal performed *puja* for the *sri chakra* he had made out of the 300 gold sovereigns during the *Navaratri* festival.

Mahalinga Pandaram who everyday massages Swami's body with ghee found that the divide on Swamigal's back had come down to his arms and told the other devotees about this. The devotees feared this was an indication of the Swamigal's last days on earth. Therefore they tearfully expressed their fears to him. "No, no, you foolish fellows, nothing like that," he said trying to dispel their fears. That day he refused to take a bath. Next day very early in the morning, his closest devotee, Ramalinga Iyer had a dream. The Swami was sitting with his *ghee*-massaged body and was throwing sand over himself. He was woken from this dream with the voice of the Swamigal calling him. He asked him to massage his hips. While doing so, Ramalinga Iyer told him about the dream "This is the work of that naughty little girl." He replied laughing. Apparently he meant Bala Tripura Sundari Ambal. This was his manner of speaking.

All this was during *Navaratri*, and on the ninth day which was *Saraswati Puja* day, it was 2 O'clock by the time the elaborate *puja* ended.

Ramalinga Iyer hurriedly took a glass of milk and went upstairs where the Swamigal was. He found him in deep sleep. All his efforts to wake him to partake of the milk were of no avail. He then forcibly tried to pour some milk into his mouth. He was able to feed him thus twice, the third time the milk spilled out. He was able to gently prop him up in a sitting position, but there was no sign of breathing. A learned Guri Tejur Subramanya Shastri had come for the *Navaratri* celebrations. They sent for him. He knew about Kuzhanthaiyanandar Swamigal, his divine birth, his greatness and also about his three *samadhi*s.

He looked at Swamigal and said "Our Swamigal has attained *moksha*," we should now perform the rites due to a great saint according to the *Paramahamsa Shastras*.

The question arose as to where should the *samadhi* be erected. Each one gave his opinion. The Mittadhar Sri Kanakasabapathy Chettiar wanted the *samadhi* to be in the land owned by him. Eventually it was decided to write down the various places being considered on small chits and pick one as the divine will of Swamigal. The chit that was picked specified that in Arasadi there was a place exclusively for the *samadhi* of saints and Sri Swamigal's resting place should be there. Shri Ramalinga Iyer undertook all the expenses and the arrangements for the Vedic rites and rituals.

On *Vijayadashami* day, after all the rituals were over at 10 O'clock in a flower decorated palanquin carried by devotees that divine body was covered with flowers. Madurai Ponnusamy Pillai played the *nadasvaram*. The palanquin was taken in a procession around the four main streets of Madurai. The *samadhi* pit was prepared filled with *vibhuti* (sacred ash), camphor, and incense, and the body was laid to rest and the pit covered. The devotees contributed generously to make this a grand ceremony for their beloved Swamigal. Mazhavanenthal Subramanya Shastri installed a *sri chakra* on the *samadhi*. A temple was built over it and in 1934 the *Kumbhabhishekam* (consecration) was performed.

Sri Kuzhanthaiyanandar Swamigal was a great saint and a great *siddha purusha*. One cannot describe his appearance. As Trilinga Swami he had a broad forehead, deepset eyes and a prominent nose. As Kuzhanthaiyanandar he had a narrow jutting forehead, beady eyes but the eyes shone, radiating divinity, he had a huge tummy and thin legs. His speech was that of a child in lisping tone — perhaps that is what gave him the name Kuzhanthaiyanandar. The *animadhi ashta siddhis* (the eight kinds of divine powers), were child's play for him.

Like the great Seshadri Swami of Tiruvannamalai he would appear before his devotees at different places. Sometimes his body would be so light that even a ten-year old child could carry him upstairs. Sometimes his body was so heavy that even strong wrestlers could not lift him. He never belonged to one place. He could be anywhere, in a hut among the poor or in a palace. He would sometimes sit in the kitchen of a house and instruct the lady of the house on how to manage a house efficiently. Next he could be imparting spiritual knowledge to *yogis*. He would never sleep during the day time, nor at night.

If he liked he would take the food offering brought by a devotee, or he would not even touch it. Sometimes when fruits were brought by devotees he would eat up all the fruits himself, at other times he would return the fruits to the giver. He might even throw away the whole lot. If asked why? He would answer, "they are not good." He looked and behaved like a child but his body was strong.

There are many stories of the lilas of Swamigal. But only a few are being written in this short narrative.

Once when he was a little child left by his parents in the temple of Meenakshi, he was found climbing onto Devi, removing her ornaments and flower garland and playfully putting his arms around her. A government official who had come there for worship got very angry that a child was allowed into the *garbha-griha* of Ambal, and ordered that the child be bodily lifted and thrown out. The devotees respectfully conveyed the fact that this child was brought up by Meenakshi Ambal herself. Not believing that such a thing could be possible, he said in a mocking manner, "Oh! If that is so, can he walk across the lotus tank?" To the joyous amazement of the devotees the child ran to the tank and walked on the water to the opposite bank.

Framley, an Englishman was a magistrate in Kashi. One day he was taking a walk with his wife when the Avadhuta Swamigal came walking towards them. The *dorai* (Indians called foreigners *dorai*) in anger raised his walking stick and gave him a blow on his back. But it was the *dorai*'s wife who was writhing in pain. The Englishman asked his servants to catch hold of the Swamigal and they dragged him to Framley's bungalow and shut him up in a room. But what was amazing was that when the Englishman came out the Swamigal was walking in front of him. Now the *dorai*'s anger turned into fear. When he made enquiries about the Swamigal the local people told him that he was a great *yogi* and anyone who harmed him would come to harm.

Framley with folded hands begged forgiveness of the Swamigal. When he heard that the Swamigal had attained *samadhi* he set aside a sum of money as his contribution for the yearly *aradhana* (*samadhi* anniversary) expenses. Even today the endowment is referred to as Framley endowment.

When Sri Kuzhanthaiyanandar Swamigal lived in Madurai, Ramana Maharishi was a young boy. Venkataraman lived in a house that was four streets away. There is no mention of their having met or come in contact. The boy Venkataraman became Ramana Maharishi and was a shining beacon attracting people from all over the world. Swamigal was in Tiruparamkundram — a place near Madurai. One day at mid-night he woke up his disciple Thinniyam Subramanya Iyer and told him "Amma (the divine Mother) has asked me to convey a written message to Ramana. So take this to him and bring me his reply." The disciple left for Tiruvannamalai, handed the note to Bhagavan and brought back his reply. The devotees were curious and eager to know what the message was and what the reply was. But swamigal said "That is a divine secret, Amma has asked me not to tell anyone."

Sri Sringeri Sarada Peetham Jagadguru Sri Abhinava Narasimha Bharati Swamigal had come to Madurai. There is a very interesting story of the meeting of the two saints. One day as *Gaja Puja* was being performed in the presence of *acharya*, a voice was heard calling *acharya* by name, "Narasimha, I am hungry," and Kuzhanthaiyanandar Swamigal with his hugh belly and spindly legs walked in. Some of those present were annoyed that the Jagadguru was called by name. But Mahaswamigal with a beaming smile on his face gestured to the attendants, who quickly understanding what he meant, brought the huge balls of rice kept to be given to the elephant, and kept the food in front of Kuzhanthaiyanandar. He swallowed the balls of rice in a trice and walked away remarking "Narasimha, I am still hungry." Everyone present felt the Lord Ganapathy Himself had come and partaken of the food.

From 1926-27 Swamigal stayed for several months in Pudukottai. Sri B.V. Kameshwara Iyer and B.V. Shankara Kameswara Iyer were brothers, devotees of Devi (Devi Upasakars) and lived an austere life, almost like *rishi*s. Both of them held high positions in the government, the former was Dewan Peshkar and the latter was head of the Education Department. They were also distantly related to Swamigal.

They hailed from Vathalagundu. Swamigal used to tell them interesting stories about their ancestors. Many miracles took place in their houses. Also in Marthandapuram Agraharam in Pudukkottai there was a pious lady named Bhagavathi Ammal, who was a great devotee of Swamigal. Her devotion was extraordinary as also Swamigal's blessings for her.

For some days Swamigal stayed in the house of one Subbier. One day suddenly like a child he angrily said, "My mother hasn't come, I do not want *kanji* (gruel)," and went upstairs and bolted himself in the room. Everyone was feeling worried and sad that Swamigal had not eaten. That day no one ate food. They were sitting sorrowful. Suddenly a beautiful lady wearing a silk sari and ornaments, with flowers in her hair came in. She had a basket of fruits and a plate full of a variety of eatables. She asked them, "Has my child come?" The devotees who were sitting sad and hungry did not answer her.

She climbed the staircase and went up. After a while the people below could hear the tinkling of anklets and music. The devotees gleefully ran upstairs and tried to peep through the chinks, they couldn't see anything. They heard their Swamigal saying "Amma, go, those rogues have come up to see."

He then opened the door and came out, with a smile in his face. He told them, "Go, go and have food. My mother came and gave me a lot of goodies to eat." Everyone forgot their hunger. Instead they were angry with themselves for not recognizing that Devi herself had come as the gorgeously dressed lady.

In a place called Kanguvarpathy, there lived a distant relative of Swamigal (of course from his *purvasramam* that is before he took to the ochre robe). Swamigal had given him a *sri chakra* for worship. Devotees had darshan of Swamigal from this *sri chakra*. Some saw Brindavan. Sometimes in the middle of the night *nadasvaram* with the accompaniment of drums could be heard. Venkatarama Rao, a devotee came with some others to Madurai to ask Swamigal about this phenomenon. He replied that after two days a *bairagi sadhu* would come here, he will explain it. Just as he said, a *bairagi sadhu* appeared, Venkatarama Rao went after him. The *sadhu* sat on the river bank and wrote some words and showed them to Venkatarama Rao. Venkatarama Rao returned to Madurai and conveyed this to Swamigal that he saw the *bairagi sadhu* in Swamigal.

When Swamigal was in Madurai a group of *bairagi sadhus* from the north returning from a pilgrimage to Rameswaram, camped in Madurai. The leader of the group would go into a deep *samadhi*, but did not know how to come out of it. His disciples would shout in his ear, sometimes sprinkle water on his face. With great difficulty he would come out of his trance.

People who passed that way would watch this in amusement. One day Ramalinga Iyer was passing that way and he witnessed the efforts of the disciples to bring back their leader from his *samadhi*. Ramalinga Iyer reported this to Swamigal, who said, "Adada! He is a half-baked *yogi*, bring him to me."

Ramalinga Iyer went at once and came back with the *bairagi sadhu*. Swamigal and the *bairagi sadhu* conversed in Hindi. The Swamigal took the *sadhu*'s hand and kept it at the side of his body below the armpit and instructed him on how to come out of *samadhi*. Since the *bairagi* was also an enlightened soul he could grasp Swamigal's instructions. He was so happy and in ecstasy bent down and lifted Swamigal's feet to his eyes, and saw the birth marks of the conch and *chakra* on his feet. The *bairagi* jumping in joy said, "Aha, my God, you are here?

You left me and have come here? Now I won't leave you." and was uncontrollable in his expression of happiness mingled with tears of joy. Swamigal calmed him and told him that they would meet again soon.

Swamigal asked his disciple Seth who was the Agent of Burmah Shell, to buy tickets for the whole group to Godavari. That night Ramalinga Iyer, his mother and wife had the same dream. Swamigal is sitting in the Himalayas surrounded by the same *bairagi* group dancing around him.

Once when Swamigal was staying in Vakil Narasimha Iyer's house he kept on saying that a telegram would come to him from Rajapalayam. The next day a man came from Rajapalayam. Even though Swamigal knew about his coming he asked him, "From where are you coming? What is the matter?" The man said, "Swami I am coming from Rajapalayam. One day my cow strayed away and I went in search of it towards the hills. There I heard a voice calling me by name. In great surprise I looked in the direction from where the voice came. Again I heard a voice from a cave bidding me to come in. There I saw a *jata mukutadhari* (with hair in a knot on top of his head and a flowing beard). He said, "Swami, if you find your cow, will you do something for me?" I bowed before him and said, "Certainly, revered Swami." He then told me that in Madurai in this address there is a Swamigal named Kuzhanthaiyanandar. It is a very long time since he left us. Please ask him to come here soon." Kuzhanthaiyanandar asked his disciples to give the man a good feast, and gave him the message for the sage in Rajapalayam that he will be coming there very soon.

*Siddha*s who take birth on this earth in their lifetime achieve so much for mankind by their spiritual knowledge, spiritual powers and miracles, which ordinary people cannot achieve in several lives.

Kuzhanthaiyanandar Swamigal was different from even those *siddhas*, being the child of the Divine Mother. He was God Himself. Once when the devotees were chanting *Lalita Sahasranamam,* even before 100 names were chanted he stopped the chanting and said, "Enough, my mother's feet are aching, perform *karpura arati* for her." He then added, "When you chant prefix and end each *nama* with the holy syllable *OM*."

Swamigal seemed as if tired of all these Lilas. His fourth and final *samadhi* was in Madurai. But even though his physical body ceased to be, his spirit and his astral presence has been felt and seen by many devotees. Through the medium of Ramalinga Iyer, his closest devotee he answers queries and problems of those who believe in him.

On 11 July 1965 he manifested as a *jyoti* to all who were fortunate to be present there. In a devotee's house, on Swamigal's birth star on a Thursday, *Nakshatra Puja* was being conducted. Special *abhisheka* and *puja* for the Swamigal's *paduka*s were also performed.

The *puja* was over. Suddenly like lightning there was a flash of light almost blinding everyone. The flash continued intermittently. All those present were amazed at this miracle. At first they thought it was someone taking a photograph with a flashlight. Someone thought it was electricity. The room was filled with this continuous flash of heavenly light.

Now everyone knew it was Swamigal blessing them and they felt as if the great saint was with them. The sporadic flashes consolidated into one beam of light and ceased.

Even today in Oonjalur on the banks of the river Kaveri there is a memorial *pitam* for Swamigal. Kuzhanthaiyanandar speaks from there though a medium, and also from his *samadhi* in Arasadi and blesses his devotees, letting them know he is still with them in spirit.

10

Sri Seshadri Swamigal

In Triunvannamalai, in the temple of Arunachaleswar, in the cave of the Patala Linga, a young boy was sitting in deep meditation, oblivious of his body and his surroundings. The boy Venkataraman, later to be known as Bhagavan Sri Ramana Maharishi, had come to this place from the thousand-pillar hall, where he used to sit in meditation. Seeing a young boy with matted hair and wearing only a *kaupinam*, the local boys, mischievous by nature, threw stones and bricks at the still figure, deep in meditation and lost to the world. Disturbed by the constant torment of the boys, the young *yogi* took refuge in the patala linga cave where no one would venture as it was infested with snakes, scorpions, mice, cockroaches, spiders and all kind of poisonous insects. Children were afraid to go anywhere near the place, but here too they would slowly peep in and from a distance throw stones, and would not allow the boy to meditate in peace. The word spread around Tiruvannamalai that a young *yogi* was sitting in *samadhi* in the Patala Linga cave. People young and old came out of curiosity to see this sight. At that time one Venkatachalapathy Mudaliar who had come to bathe in the tank, saw the crowd and wanted to know the reason for this. He heard a voice laughing, *hee, hee, hee,* and following the voice, a semi-naked *swami*, wearing a dirty piece of cloth, having dirty matted hair, an unkempt beard and moustache, emerged. Mudaliar knew the *swami* to be a great saint. The *swami* picked up a brick and threw it at the crowd, and the crowd melted away. Everyone there knew

5. Sri Seshadri Svamigal.

about this *swami* and they dared not linger as they were in fear and awe of him. The *swami* then addressed Mudaliar and said, "I am Parvati — you know me don't you? My son Subramanya is doing *tapas* inside that cave. Come I will show him to you." So saying he caught hold of the Mudaliar's hand and went down the steps. Mudaliar could see a head behind the *Shivalinga*. He was frightened and went back and brought some men with him. They went into the cave and bodily lifted the boy and brought him out. The whole body was covered with dust and dirt, in both the thighs centipedes, cockroaches, and scorpions had eaten into the flesh and made deep wounds. The *swami* said, "Do you see my son Subramanya? Hee, hee, I am Parvati. See how absorbed he is in meditation?" From that day, the boy's needs were attended to. The Swamigal used to bring the food he had begged from various homes and forcibly feed the young *yogi*. He stood guard with a stick to drive away the curious and idle crowd of school children. Thus the older Swamigal served the boy *swami*. Who were these two?

The young *swami* was later to be known all over the world as Bhagavan Ramana Maharishi and the older *swami* was Sri Seshadri Swamigal. If Seshadri Swamigal had not saved the young *yogi* from the cave of the Patala Linga, perhaps the world might not have come to know of Ramana Maharishi. Seshadri Swamigal was called the elder brother and Ramana Maharishi his younger brother, their relationship was a spiritual one.

Adi Shankaracharya after establishing the four *mutt*s — Sringeri, Dwarka, Puri and Jyotirmath — came eventually to Kancheepuram. He installed the *sri chakra* in the Kamakshi Amman temple *garbha-griha* (*sanctum sanctorum*). He needed *pundit*s who were Sri Vidya *upasaka*s and knew the Devi *puja-vidhi*. But he could not find suitable *pundit*s for the performance of the daily *puja*. He continued his journey and came to the river Narmada on the banks of which there was a village inhabited by brahmins. All of them were Sri Vidya *upasakas*. He selected thirty families and requested them to settle in Kancheepuram, and take charge of the worship of Devi Kamakshi. These thirty families settled in Kancheepuram and generations of them were carrying on the temple worship. There were many scholars among them and *gurus*, who had disciples, all well versed in the Shastras and the Sri Vidya *puja-vidhi*. These families were called Kamakotis. Centuries later, these scholarly families became almost extinct, leaving only two Kamakoti families in Kancheepuram. These two families, between themselves, carried on the *Puja* at the Kamakshi temple, combining scriptural knowledge with utmost devotion. In those days, the Shaivites and Vaishnavites were bitterly fighting each other. The Shaivites were devotees of Shiva and Vaishnavites were devotees of Vishnu. As if ordained by god with a mission to bring harmony among the warring sectarian groups, a great scholar named Kamakoti Sastrigal was born in a family of Devi *upasakas*. Kamakoti Shastrigal and his wife had one daughter. He also looked after his younger brother's family like his own. Kamakoti Shastrigal was often compared to the great scholar Appayya Dikshitar. His knowledge of the Vedas and Shastras was unparalleled. He was a great musician and had composed musical compositions in Telugu and Sanskrit. His younger brother's daughter Maragatham was a quick learner and brilliant in her studies. Kamakoti Shastrigal therefore imparted Sanskritic knowledge and music to her.

Maragatham's uncle, Kamakoti Shastri was now on the look out for a suitable bridegroom for her. His choice fell on Varadarajan from among one of the families there. He was a handsome youth and had studied Sanskrit and astrology under eminent scholars. Maragatham and Varadarajan were a perfect match in everyway. The wedding was celebrated and the couple lived an ideal life. But even after many years of marriage there were no children. They went on a pilgrimage to Rameswaram where childless couples go, hoping for special blessings, since this pilgrimage is believed to bestow the blessings of an offspring. They gave generously for charity and performed *dosha pariharam*s (the performance of penances to ward of the evil effects of hostile planets). But their desire was not fulfilled. Kamakoti Shastrigal was very much affected by the misery of Maragatham and her husband. He prayed to Devi and with his heart full of devotion, prayed to her to bless the couple with a child. Devi Kamakshi appeared to him in a dream and said, "They should come here, and my son chant the *mantra*s with the fingers placed in butter for forty days and let the couple have the butter everyday." Kamakoti Shastrigal asked Maragatham and Varadarajan to stay with him. For forty days he gave them the sanctified butter to eat. Soon after the forty days of prayer were over, Maragatham conceived.

It was the auspicious month of Thai — corresponding to the English month between the middle of January to the middle of February. It was on *shashti,* the sixth day after the full moon, under the birth star Hastam — and the day was Saturday, 22 January 1870 — that a son was born to Maragatham and Varadarajan. The child was given the name Seshadri. The child was beautiful and as he grew up he would sit and listen to his father teaching his students. When his father sat for his daily worship and chanting, the boy would imitate him, doing all that he did. Once, when Seshadri was perhaps three or four years old, his mother holding him by the hand, was walking to the Varadaraja Perumal Temple. It was a festival day and the streets were lined with vendors and peddlers selling their wares to the crowds going to the temple. Even today one can see a permanent bazaar in front of any big temple, and on festival days the shops could be much more in number. As Maragatham was walking the little boy Seshadri pulled her *sari* and wanted her to stop. He then pointed to a man who had a huge pile of brass images of Lord Krishna, and wanted one. The looks of the child and the way he asked his mother appealed so much to the seller that he said, "child, here take any one of these for yourself. You are my first customer." With his mother's permission, the boy ran his hand over the entire lot and took out one Krishna idol. Maragatham was amused and smiling took out money to pay the vendor. He refused the payment. The child went happily, hugging the idol to his chest.

The next day Maragatham was going to the temple and when she came to the place where the seller of the Krishna idols was sitting, he got up and came running and fell full length prostrating before her.

Maragatham was taken aback. Standing up with folded hands the vendor said, "Mother, your son is a divine child since he has a golden hand. He touched my wares with his hands, and all the idols — a thousand — were sold out yesterday. What can I say about this miracle? Previously whenever I came to sell my idols, I could not sell more than twenty or thirty, and now the whole lot of one thousand idols was sold in a short time. Your child is lord Krishna." As he said this, his eyes were full of tears. The mother felt very proud and hugged her son. From that day he earned the epithet "Thangakai Seshadri" meaning "Seshadri with the golden touch." When Seshadri was five years old, his father performed his *aksharabhyasa*, literally marking his entry into the world of letters. He was sent to study in the Sanskrit *gurukula* (ancient term for school system) and Tamil in the temple school. When Seshadri was seven or eight he had gained so much proficiency in these two subjects that he would hold the attention of an audience consisting mostly of young children, with his discourses.

In his seventh year his grand uncle Kamakoti Shastrigal performed his *upanayanam* (sacred thread ceremony marking the boy's entry into the domain of education). He sent him to the temple *pathashala* (school) to study the Vedas. Seshadri learnt Nyaya Shastra from a Madhva (sect founded by Madhvacharya which believes in the doctrine of dualism) *guru*. Another *guru* taught him grammar and commentaries on the major texts. Thus he was given extensive training in all aspects of the Shastras. In course of time he attained such proficiency that even in institutions of higher learning with a large public in attendance, he would be requested to speak.

One day Seshadri was called by his father to come near and sit by him. Seshadri was at that time twelve years old. Sri Varadarajan put his arms around the boy and tears were pouring down his cheeks. Maragatham saw this and sensing something serious, came running and crying aloud. Nearby relatives came and calmed her and dispelled her anxiety. But both Varadarajan and Maragatham could not control their tears. Varadarajan took control of himself and kissing his son on the forehead sent him to school. Next day he got up as usual, finished his routine of *puja* and prayers and went to the temple of Kamakshi. He was there for a long time praying. That night around midnight, the disease *adhisaram* (a form of diarrohea or dysentery that usually afflicts those who indulge in penance and meditation) that was destroying him, suddenly flared up. Now everyone understood why he was so grief-stricken.

Maragatham was in a shocked state. Varadarajan called his wife and son to him, and with tears streaming they stood by his bedside, "My son. Do not weep. This disease they call *adhisaram* will never cause loss of memory or consciousness which is why *yogi*s welcome this disease," he told them. "I have something to tell you. In a little while from now this body will cease to exist. Remember my son, however much knowledge you might gain through study, only practical knowledge will serve you." Thus he gave his son a parting message from his deathbed and breathed his last. Seshadri trembled with grief. What was to be done? The death of his father affected him very much. Unbearable grief at his father's death, combined with his spiritual quest, appears to be the cause for his renunciation.

As soon as he heard the sad news, Kamakoti Shastrigal came and after the funeral rites were over, took his beloved Maragatham, Seshadri and his younger brother Narasimhan with him to his house.

Kamakoti Shastrigal noticed that Seshadri was always immersed in deep meditation and inclined to the spiritual in his aspirations. Kamakoti Shastrigal gave him *jnanopadesham* (spiritual initiation) and thus became his first *guru*.

Many high officials came to Kamakoti Shastrigal for getting initiated with a *mantra* and for gaining spiritual knowledge. Shastrigal would ask Seshadri to take classes for them. Sir C.P. Ramaswamy Iyer's grandmother used to come to listen to Seshadri's discussion on the *Ramayana* and *Srimad Bhagavatam*.

One day Kamakoti Shastrigal was down with shivering and fever. He was bedridden for nearly three months and felt that his end was near. As it was the practice of taking *apat sannyasa* before death came, Kamakoti Shastrigal took *apat sannyasa* (literally meaning *sannyasa* in the face of imminent death) from one Sri Krishnananda Swamigal of Brahma Mutt in Kanjeepuram and was given the name Brahmananda Saraswati. He now left his home and stayed in the temple of Chakrathalwar. Maragatham would visit him and give him *bhiksha*. After that he went to a place called Thamal. Within ten days of going there he attained *samadhi*. His *athishthanam* (final resting place) is on the bank of the river Sarpa and can be seen even today. Maragatham felt this loss very keenly. She felt orphaned without Kamakoti *Shastrigal*'s support.

Seshadri was now seventeen years old. In knowledge, wisdom and good looks he was outstanding. He also learnt music from his mother and became a very good singer. But Maragatham after her husband's death had lost interest in life. She now wanted to see her eldest son Seshadri married and be relieved of all her domestic duties. She had chosen Kakini Devi, the daughter of her husband's sister, as a suitable wife for him. It was all decided among the elders. But fate and God willed otherwise.

Seshadri had an uncle, his father's younger brother Ramaswamy Iyer. He and his wife Kalyani had no issue, and they loved Seshadri and Narasimhan and looked upon them as their own children. This uncle was a great astrologer. For that matter, everyone in the Kamakoti family knew some astrology. Ramaswamy Iyer compared the horoscope of Seshadri and his sister Lakshmi's daughter Kakini Devi. As he looked into Seshadri's horoscope, his face became grave. He tried to hide his feelings, but felt that he had to tell them the truth. He told his sister, "Lakshmi, this marriage will not take place and even if it does, your daughter will not live with her husband. This boy has *parivraja yoga* in his horoscope and that means he will soon become a renunciate — *a sannyasi*. His planetary positions clearly indicate this. So please abandon this proposal and look for another alliance for your daughter."

His blunt and unpalatable prediction annoyed his sister and other relatives, and they refused to heed his negative astrology. But he knew that what he said was the truth and nothing could change that and no one had the courage to defy him. Lakshmi settled another boy for her daughter and thus Seshadri was saved from an embarrassing situation. Now that the only desire she had of seeing her son married was not to be, Maragatham completely immersed herself in prayers. She lost interest in food and would eat only to sustain her body. She had an attack of high fever, which may have been diagnosed as typhoid by an allopathic doctor, but no doctor was called. Maragatham had a premonition that her end had come. Her health steadily deteriorated. She called her sons to her. Strangely, she put her hand on Seshadri's chest and hit it three times, as if she gave up all her desires for him and was preparing him for a different life. She asked Seshadri to sing a composition of Kamakoti Shastrigal beginning with "Amba Sive." As he sang, she joined him. She uttered loudly three times, "Arunachala, Arunachala, Arunachala" and placing her head on Seshadri's lap breathed her last. Seshadri fainted and lost consciousness. This was the end of worldly life for him. The slender thread, which was his attachment to his mother, had snapped. He performed a son's duties towards his mother. Seshadri's uncle Ramaswamy Iyer and his aunt legally adopted Narasimhan, younger brother of Seshadri.

After the passing away of his mother, Seshadri was drawn more and more into meditation and contemplation. The last word of his mother "Arunachala" was ever ringing in his ears, and his mind dwelt in contemplation of Arunachala Jyoti. So he drew the five peaks of Arunachala and along with it placed the picture of Sri Kamakshi and the picture of Sri Rama and spent hours in worship. As days went, the *puja* hours became longer. If he started his *puja* at seven in the morning inside the room with the door closed he would come out at 1 o'clock. Sometimes his aunt would loudly ask him to open the door and keep banging on the door. Sometimes while sleeping he would loudly recite the *Durga Suktam*. He would call out loud "Sonadrinatha"! His behaviour became noticeably peculiar. He would sit in front of the Chakrathalwar Sannadhi and do japam for hours. Sometimes he could be seen wandering here and there in the night. If someone asked him, "Seshadri what japam are you repeating?" He would answer "I am uttering the *mantra* Ambasyapare from *Narayana Upanishad,* like *kamokarshit manyurakarshit, kamaha karoti naham karomi.* 'I have reached one lakh, I have to repeat half a lakh times more."

People began to talk of him as the mad Seshadri. The love his uncle and aunt and relatives and friends had for him made them talk about him with concern. This made him feel chained by their love, not free to roam about at will. He therefore without anyone knowing went in the night to the cremation ground and there continued his japas. By constant meditation, his *kundalini* was aroused. He experienced the bliss of self-realization. Seshadri found the interference from his family stifling, as some even raised the issue of marriage once again saying, "if we somehow got him married this madness would stop." Seshadri who can now be referred to as Swamigal spoke to them and quoted from the Shastras to explain to them his state of mind. He decided he should go away from Kancheepuram. He also felt that Arunachala was beckoning him but thought that he should first take sanyas from a *guru*. An opportunity soon presented itself.

Seshadri Swamigal has gone to the temple of Vishwanath and there he saw a *sannyasi* who belonged to the Gaudiya sect sitting with four disciples in front of him. When he saw this scene, Seshadri Swamigal believed that it was Lord

Dakshinamurty sitting under the peepal tree with his four disciples, who had come to initiate him into sanyas. He recited the *Dakshinamurty Ashtakam* slowly with copious tears flowing from his eyes and paid obeisance before the *sannyasi*. The *sannyasi* at once recognized the spiritual greatness of this youth and said, "my child, do not feel sad, you will get what you want," and made him sit near him. Seshadri Swamigal confided in him and told him of his desire to get *sannyasa* from him. From that day the *guru* had five disciples. The *guru* observed his new disciple and found him ripe for taking *sannyasa*. On an auspicious day, the *guru* conferred *sannyasa* on Seshadri and initiated him in the *sannyasa dharma*. Seshadri Swamigal absorbed all that the *guru* taught him. After some time he went to the river and discarded the emblems of *dhanda* and *kamandalu*, and went on his wanderings. It seemed as if the Gaudiya Swamigal came to Kancheepuram only to give *sannyasa* to Seshadri, as he also left the place soon afterwards. Seshadri Swamigal never went back to his native town of Kancheepuram.

The death anniversary or *shraddha* ceremony of his mother was to be performed. His aunt Kalyani was lamenting that Seshadri had not come home. She was nagging her husband and pleading with him to find Seshadri and bring him home. Seshadri Swami's uncle Ramaswamy Iyer went out in search of him and after a tiring search found him and brought him home. They locked him up in a room, but the Swamigal kept quiet and did not say anything. The *shraddham* ceremony was performed. It was important that the children and close relatives partake of the food offered to the departed. The Swami's uncle and aunt wanted Seshadri to at least partake of the food and opened the door and called out to him but there was obviously no sound since he was not there. In agitation they went inside the room and examined the windows; the iron bars were intact. His uncle called aloud, "my son, Seshadri where have you gone?" and in agony sat down on the floor holding his head. All the relatives and friends joined in the search for the Swamigal. As days went by they lost all hope of finding him. Some said, "I saw him here," others said, "I saw him there," but he was nowhere to be seen.

Seshadri Swamigal escaped from everyone and went to a place called Kaveripakkam and stayed in the local Shiva temple. His mother's sister (Kamakoti Shastrigal's daughter) lived in Kaveripakkam. Her son Seshayyar had come to the temple. Seeing Seshadri Swamigal he called out, "Anna (brother), you are here," and ran home to give the news. His aunt and uncle came and asked him to come home, but the Swamigal refused. They then brought *bhiksha* for him there. He stayed there for three or four days. One day his brother Seshayyar was sitting with him and saw a serpent creeping towards Seshadri Swamigal. Seshayyar shouted, "Anna, snake, snake." Swamigal saw the snake and said, "come, come near me." The snake glided onto his arm and made its way upwards and coiled around his neck and lifted its hood and was swaying in a snake dance. Seshayyar shouting the news "Anna was bitten by a snake" ran home. The snake after a few minutes came down and went away. A crowd gathered and saw the Swamigal in a yogic pose and they prostrated before him. The news reached Kancheepuram and uncle Ramaswamy Iyer and aunt Kalyani came post-haste to Kaveripakkam and saw Swamigal in the Shiva temple. They begged, pleaded and cajoled him to return home, but the Swamigal was firm in his resolve and refused. The uncle and aunt stayed for some days there and had the satisfaction of taking *bhiksha* for their beloved Seshadri, and returned to Kancheepuram.

One day, Swamigal quietly left the place and avoiding the roads, walked through the jungles and through small hamlets and in the middle of 1889 reached Arunachala or Tiruvannamalai. He was then only nineteen years old. He spent forty years in Tiruvannamalai performing innumerable miracles. By merely looking at a person, the Swamigal bestowed his grace on him and spiritually transformed him. By a mere touch he could heal. He behaved like a madman, but the people of Tiruvannamalai knew that he was an extraordinary saint.

The meeting of the two saints — Seshadri Swamigal and Ramana Maharishi — has been described in the very beginning of this narrative. Seshadri Swamigal was referred to as the elder brother of Ramana Maharishi.

Ramakrishna Paramahamsa preached that the development of a saint is said to be in seven phases. The first three phases consist of *sadhana*s meaning intense spiritual practices; the fourth phase is Brahmavit. The fifth, sixth and seventh phases are Brahmavitvaran, Brahmavitvariyan and Brahmavarishta. Seshadri Swamigal moved between the last three phases. Once a saint is fixed in the seventh phase called Brahmavarishta it means his final *samadhi* is near. In that state the body remains on the earth for only twenty-one days. Then like a dry branch or ripe fruit (*urvarukamiva*) it falls off. But there are some saints who transcend all these phases. They are born on earth to guide and bless those who are spiritual seekers in need of a helping hand. Our Seshadri Swamigal was such an avatar who had come into the world to bless people and guide them. What kind of a person was Seshadri Swamigal, how did he look? As a child he was handsome but as he grew older, he discarded everything and was abnormal in his habits. This sometimes meant not bathing nor bothering to cut his hair which was matted, wearing almost nothing except for a small piece of cloth which was usually unwashed and dirty. In fact, he broke all the rules of normal behaviour.

He was of medium height and his eyes were mostly half closed. If he only opened his eyes and looked at a person that person would receive great spiritual blessings. Seshadri Swamigal had many many followers. They would bring him a new cloth to wear but the next minute he would hang it on a donkey's neck or drag it in the dust and the colour would change from white to red. Sometimes he wore a single *dhoti* reaching up to his toes and another across his chest like the sacred thread of a brahmin. If anybody gave him food, he would eat just two hands full and the rest he would scatter all round him. After eating he would wipe his hands on his *dhoti* and walk away at a great speed. Even if one were to run behind him in order to catch up with him, it would not be possible because his walking speed was so fast. While sitting he would very easily sit on his heels adopting the *svastikasana*. It is not humanly possible to adopt that posture for a length of time. If someone were to ask him, "Swami, please sing a song" he would sing the Pallavi and get up and go away. But that short piece of music would be so divinely melodious. Some-times sitting on his cot he would play the *mridangam jati* (beats of the percussion instrument). The rhythm would be so enchanting that the listeners would lose themselves in it, but suddenly it would stop.

For Seshadri Swamigal to whom *siddhis* came naturally, anything and everything was possible. Seshadri Swamigal's behavioural pattern was very, very strange. He would enter a shop or any side hotel. If it were a shop he would scatter the items all over, throwing them from the shelf, and if it were an eating-house, he would scatter the sweets and the savouries all around. He would open the cash box, take out the cash and strew it all around. But strangely the owners were very happy when he entered their shop or hotel and did these strange things. They knew that he was *Thanga kai Seshadri*

Swamigal. When he did this their fortunes were made. Others would also want him to come to their establishments, but no one dared to call him. They could only pray he would come. If someone not knowing the ways of Seshadri Swamigal were to ask him to come to his shop or hotel he would heap abuse on him and if had a stick or a brick, he would throw it at him. But even those he abused or hurt only benefited from his presence as they were also blessed by his grace.

He would go to an oil mongers shop, dip into the oil barrels and pour oil on himself and walk out with oil dropping from his head and body for months. When it rained Seshadri Swamigal was in his element. He would sit in the puddles of water and laugh and enjoy himself. He would never dry himself. Once in a while he would ask the barber to shave him but before the barber could complete his task, he would run off with a partly shaved chin and would be seen in this state for months. It seemed as if he had conquered hunger, thirst, sleep, sadness, desire, even old age and death.

There was a beggar named Manikkasami who was devoted to Seshadri Swamigal. Whatever food this beggar brought by begging was very much liked by Swamigal. Manikkasami never ate without first feeding Swamigal. Sometimes Swamigal would disappear for three or four days, Manikkasami also would not take food. Once Swamigal came back after three days, took the stale and foul smelling food from the beggar's bowl and ate it with great relish.

One constant habit of his was to come back to the Arunachaleswar Temple where the God Kambathu Nayanar shrine was and rest there. Kambathu Nayanar was Murugan etched in one of the pillars. A mattress and two pillows were permanently spread there for him. A man, innocently trapped in a court case, donated this as because of Swamigal's grace he was exonerated of the charges, and he got back his money. This mattress was in a filthy condition with mud and dust and this was where he ate the three-day-old food brought by the beggar.

Swamigal sometimes spoke in conundrums. No one could understand what he meant, but to those who were close to him the meaning would be clear — they may be prophetic or philosophical, but from the sound of it, one would think it was nonsense. His words remind one of the medieval mystic poets like Kabir and Muktā Bai. Here is one example of Seshadri Swamigal's utterances: "A man wants a wife. Here are ten people, an elephant comes and stands. Even if the one who went to Kashi returns, is there any answer? Mm; Mm . . ." The explanation to these seemingly disjointed statements has not been given by anyone. Some revealing statements about Seshadri Swamigal were made by Bhagavan Ramana. Ramana Maharishi had come down from Skandashramam to stay in an *ashram* built at the site where his mother Alagammal's *samadhi* was. When a sofa was brought for Ramana Maharishi to sit in a reclining position, the devotees were in doubt whether he would agree to sit on it and came prepared to plead with him to have this comfort. As soon as he saw the sofa, Ramana Maharishi said, "I know this is brought here for my comfort. There is no need to persuade me. Am I like Seshadri who is in a half-conscious state?"

Although saints are all self-realized souls who attained the highest form of divinity by becoming one with the spiritual fountainhead, in form and in their spiritual manifestations they were of different kinds. Some lived alone away from their fellow human beings, some saints wandered in the forests and mountains and made their abode there. There are some saints who have lived among people as ordinary persons and have yet attained *moksha* through their divinity. Some saints observed silence, some behaved like madmen. Some saints like Kabir could carry on their work and be still detached and were self-realized saints. Seshadri Swamigal acted like a madman for forty years, but was a saint whom the people loved and worshipped. Countless are the *lilas* he has performed. His whole life was a divine play.

Let me end the account of this unusual saint with a few stories about him. Murugan was a cart driver; he was slavishly devoted to Seshadri Swamigal. Seshadri Swamigal used to ride in his cart many times. There came a time when his earnings were so meagre he could hardly have one meal a day and was feeling very depressed. Suddenly Seshadri Swamigal went to his house and asked for gruel. He drank all the gruel there and while leaving said, "go, sell your bull and cart and go away." It was a great surprise for Murugan when a businessman from Madras who was of his caste came to his house and offered his daughter in marriage to him. He went with his wife and in-laws to Madras. He was now the son-in-law of a prosperous businessman and had no use for his cart or bull.

An incident happened which proved that Bhagavan Ramana and Seshadri Swamigal were one. There was a devotee named M.K. Subramanya Shastri in Ramanashramam. One day he asked Bhagavan a strange question, stating his problem about the lack of concentration during meditation, "Bhagavan they say that if one has Purnadhi Lehiyam, one's mind can concentrate and meditation will be easy. Can I have it?" Bhagavan Ramana said, "No, not at all." But Subramanya Iyer who was firmly convinced by someone that he should eat the Lehiyam and it would definitely help him, had a good dose of it. The only effect it had was dangerous as he felt as if the sky and earth were revolving. He went out for some fresh air and as he came out, he saw Seshadri Swamigal going past and sitting on the verandah of a house. A few people were near him; Subramanya Shastri also went and bowed before him. The Swamigal told him immediately, "Never, never, I told you not to eat the Lehiyam did I not?" The man bent his head in shame. How did Swamigal know what Ramana Maharishi had told him? Were Bhagavan and Swamigal one and the same?

Kavyakhanda Ganapathy Shastrigal, who was called Naina by everyone, was a very great scholar and gave discourses on *Ramayana, Mahabharata, Bhagavad-Gita* and other Puranic texts. He was also a great devotee of Ramana; it was Kavyakhanda Ganapathy Shastrigal who gave Ramana the nomenclature "Bhagavan Ramana Maharishi." There was no one who did not know him. He also spoke about the greatness and divinity of Seshadri Swamigal.

Once Kavyakhanda Ganapathy Shastrigal was giving a discourse. The people gathered there collected Rs. 50 to be presented to him as a token. At that time Seshadri Swamigal happened to come there and the organizer handed over the money to Swamigal. Previously on such occasions when he was given the money intended for the scholar he would throw it in all the four corners and walk away. That day when he was given the money he asked, "What is this money for?" They replied that he could give it to whomsoever he pleased. Swamigal gave the sum of Rs. 50 to Naina chanting a *shloka*.

वागर्थ इति, संपृक्तौ वागर्थ प्रतिपद्धये ।
जगतः पितरौ वन्दे पार्वती परमेश्वरौ ॥

vaagartha iti sampriktau vagartha pratipaddhaye ।
jagatah pitarau vande parvati parameshwarau ॥

Parvati and Parameshwara (Shiva), the father and mother of the universe, they who are like the word and its meaning, who reveal to us the word and its meaning; to them, I bow!

He said, "Give this to your son who is getting married." The people around were amazed at this gesture of Swamigal. In subtle ways, Seshadri Swamigal would reveal his knowledge of the past, present and future.

Vallimalai Swamigal who was known as Tirupugazh Swami came to Tiruvannamalai in search of a *guru*. He had heard of Seshadri Swamigal and wanted him to be his *guru*. Swamigal had neither seen him before nor did he know his name. He also did not know that he was known as Tirupugazh Swamigal. When Vallimalai Swamigal requested Swamigal to accept him as his disciple, Swamigal spontaneously said, "Tirupugazh is your *guru*, do not leave it, you have been a *sannyasi* for many generations." Tirupugazh Swami was surprised that Swamigal knew that there was a *sannyasi* in every generation of his family. Swamigal could command rainfall. If anyone was bitten by a scorpion, he would take some sand and repeat some *mantra* and put it on the bitten place and immediately the pain would go. He would sometimes entertain devotees with his *siddhi*s. He told a devotee that he could show her Indraloka and when she showed disbelief he showed her Indraloka in a flash. Echammal was privileged to see him in a death-like *samadhi* state for eight hours. In this way Seshadri Swamigal was a living miracle for forty years.

Perhaps he was eventually tired of these miracles and of life on this earth. In 1929 in the Tamil month of Kartikai (middle of November to middle of December) he decided that it was time he chose to enter his eternal *samadhi* but he wanted the permission of his divine mother. For Swamigal all women were mother Raja Rajeshwari. So he went to a devotee named Subbulakshmi and in his usual cryptic manner of speech, asked her, "Subbulakshmi, I have been wanting to ask you something for a long time. I'm disgusted with this world because the people here trouble me too much. Shall I build a new house and do *yogabhyasa*?" She did not catch the inner meaning of his words. "Yes, one who does know to tie the cloth around his waist properly but lets it slip, who cannot even eat the food obtained by begging, you are thinking of building a house. Great!!" she said mockingly. But Swamigal came to her house everyday and asked the same question. This became a daily routine. It then occurred to her that there must be some hidden meaning in this question. So one day in answer to his routine question she gave the answer, "Alright. Do not pester me. Go and build your house and do *yogabhyasa*." Swamigal was triumphant that he had got Para-Shakti's permission. After that he never went anywhere near her house.

It is a great irony that saints suffer due to the love of people and even their end is because of the excessive love of devotees for the *guru*. Ramana's small lump below his left elbow caused him itching and he scratched it. A devotee who had noticed him scratching, immediately asked with concern as to what was causing the itching. Bhagavan pointed to the lump. As days and months passed, the lump grew bigger and it was decided to ask a devotee to examine it. X-ray and blood tests were taken and a small bit of the lump was sent for biopsy. It was diagnosed as a cancerous growth. The team of doctors was of the opinion that it should be operated upon and removed. Bhagavan told them to leave things alone and that there was no need for any operation, but now the devotees of the *ashram* and the doctors decided that the lump should be removed. Ultimately the lump surfaced again, after which three operations were done and Bhagavan became very weak. But he never complained of pain or discomfort but was his usual calm self. Till the end he insisted on giving *darshana* to devotees, smiling his divine smile. On a personal note, my mother, K. Anandammal, was among that last line of devotees, who had his *darshana* and saw the *jyoti* that flashed across the sky like a shooting meteor, which was visible in many parts of India. Since the Ramana Jyoti left the body, one wonders and ponders on the words of Bhagavan when he said, "Let it be, there is no need to operate." If only the devotees had the wisdom to understand Bhagavan and left the wound untouched, who knows it might have got cured.

In a very similar way, the devotees of Seshadri Swamigal wanted to perform *abhishekam* for him. Swamigal said, "No, no, if you perform *abhishekam* I will get fever." But the sweet, childlike saint Seshadri Swamigal was made to sit and pose for a photograph while cold water and rose water from several pitchers were poured on his head in the name of *abhishekam*. A garland of flowers adorned his neck, and a picture was taken.

There was a long queue of devotees waiting to take turns to pour the specially brought water from Shivaganga. The *abhishekham* stopped only when the water was exhausted. Just as the Swamigal had predicted, that night he developed very high fever. But was Swamigal one to be afraid of fever? He, as usual, went about roaming the streets and scattering his blessings by his miracles.

At that time a Salem advocate B.V. Narasimha Iyer happened to be there. He sent a telegram to Kuzhumani Narayana Sastrigal to come immediately. He came with fruits and a shawl, and at once went to see Swamigal and weeping sat near and peeled an orange for him. Swamigal took the peeled orange and squeezing it threw it away. Subbalakshmi Ammal came there and when he saw her Swamigal said, "Now do you understand? Can you see what is happening?" and smiled a beatific smile. She wept uncontrollably. Doctors were brought to see him but Swamigal was adamant, and did not take any medicine. That day it had rained. In the evening Swamigal slowly got up, put his arm around Narayana Shastri's neck and went with him to Shivaganga. There among the trees was a pit filled with water. Swamigal lay down in the water. The shawl with which Shastri had covered him was muddy; he was lying there till three in the morning. 4-1-1929 was a Friday. As the day dawned, Swamigal bade farewell one by one to his limbs. He held his last breath, his face suddenly brightened and in a state of complete bliss, his breathing stopped.

All around people were waiting, some were comforting the weeping ones, and some were singing *bhajans*. Swamigal's body was bathed, decorated and on the banks of Agni *thirtham* they performed his *samadhi* rites. Bhagavan Sri Ramana Maharishi came to bid farewell to his elder brother. The *jyoti*, which had illumined Arunachala, now was extinguished in Arunachala.

Seshadri Swamigal had only shed his earthly body and his spirit still lives on amidst his beloved devotees. In Arasady from the samadhi of Kuzhanthaiyanandar Swamigal and at Kodumudi on the banks of Kaveri in Oonjalur and Coimbatore, Seshadri Swamigal speaks to his devotees and answers their questions through a medium. Kovai E.S. Sivaramakrishnan has the good fortune to be the medium through whom Swamigal communicates. Not only Seshadri Swamigal but Kuzhanthaiyanandar Swamigal, Sadashiva Brahmendar and Shirdi Sai Baba also communicate through him. People come in hundreds to his house in Coimbatore.

Although they all bear the nomenclature "Saint" each one of them is different and also the same. The methods and process may be different but the result is the same. They were all *jivan mukta*s — that is they attained *mukti* or self-realization while they were living. The birth cycle of birth and death, which is inevitable for all human beings to work out their *karma*, till, in some distant millennium, they attain salvation, does not apply to *jivan mukta*s as their cycle ended with this saintly birth.

The lives of these saints reveal that the path of each one was tortuous; God makes them go through fire before they reach the ultimate goal. Blessed are we that such saints walked this earth like ordinary mortals.

6. Sri Swayam Prakasa Svamigal.

11

Sri Swayam Prakasa Swamigal

For a person who has attained the state of bliss which comes through God realization there is no worldly attachment. He can continue doing his duty, doing whatever work he is assigned, with diligence and excellence without any attachment. Brother Lawrence worked as a cook. He was an excellent cook, and kept the kitchen clean, but his heart and mind belonged to Jesus. So also was Sri Krishnamurthi working as a clerk in the settlement office. But today, as he came out of his office, his mind was troubled and anxiety was writ large on his face. The anxiety arose from his deep-rooted feeling that his family was trying to thrust matrimony on him.

His father and elder brother had come three years ago with a marriage proposal for him. Krishnamurthi had been firm in his resolve that he had no intention of marrying and leading the life of a householder. He had told them that he had chosen his path of devotion and service to God. But he was troubled by their reaction and the condition they had laid. They were so angered by his attitude that his father had said, "Look here, you ungrateful fellow, you think because you have an English education you have the insolence to defy your elders? If you do not agree to marry the girl we have chosen for you, return the sum of Rs 3,000 we have spent on your education — then you can do what you please." Krishnamurthi had taken up the challenge and promised them that he would return the money they had spent on him at the earliest.

He had started saving some money every month from his salary of Rs 60. In three years he had been able to save only Rs 500. How could he raise the balance of Rs 2500? On that day he had received a letter from his father that he would be coming with another proposal. This was the reason for his troubled mind and acute despondency. "How can I tackle this impediment which is standing in my way? I have surrendered myself to God, I cannot accept the proposal imposed upon me by my father, I must decide now." He suddenly became calm having come to a decision.

Just as he expected, he saw his father and elder brother waiting for him in his room. On their part they had also come with a plan. They spoke to him with affection and gentle persuasion. They reminded him that God would not approve of his hurting his parents. The present proposal they had brought was an alliance with the daughter of Paranoor Muthuswami Iyer who was very rich. The girl was beautiful and the horoscopes matched. "Give up your obstinacy and marry the girl," his father pleaded.

But Krishnamurthi remained silent unmoved by all that his father and brother said. His stony silence made his brother furious and he shouted, "your English education has made you arrogant," and seeing a jug of water there, was going to pour the water on Krishnamurthi's head. Krishnamurthi smiled and said "Ganapadigale! (a learned Sanskrit *pundit*) while you pour the water please chant the Purusha-Suktam, that will purify my mind and body." "But let me tell you," he added, "you have broken the challenge you made with me, you did not wait for me to give you the Rs. 3,000 you wanted. Here is my pass book, I have saved Rs. 500 take that and go home. Hereafter there is no bond between us, it is broken," saying that he walked out.

In this our land, in every century, in every era, saints have lived amongst us and through their knowledge and spiritual greatness inspired many aspirants to follow the spiritual path shown by these *gurus*. It is believed that God himself manifests on earth as these spiritual *gurus* to guide mankind to realize his true purpose in this world.

So also was Krishnamurthi. He was to be revered as Senthamangalam Sri Swayam Prakasa Swamigal. God had chosen him to be a spiritual *guru*.

Swamigal was born in a village called Kalpattu, 8 miles from Tirukovilur to Sri Ramaswamy Iyer and Srimati Janaki Ammal. The date of his birth was 28-11-1871 corresponding to the Tamil month Karthikai 14th and the year Prajothpati. Tirukovilur is a place where Shaivites and Vaishnavites lived in harmony. This is also where the Alwars — Poygai Alwar, Bhoothathalwar and Peyalwar — shared a space in which only one could lie down, two could sit, and three could stand. So since they were three they shared the space by standing and singing the praise of the Lord all night. Finally they felt the presence of a fourth person in their midst who was Lord Vishnu himself.

The Nayanars were devotees of Shiva. Thus in days when there was rivalry and disharmony and fighting among Vaishnavites and Shaivites, Tirukovilur stands out as a place where there was complete harmony.

Once there was a great famine in that region and many left Tirukovilur and migrated to other places. Sri Ramaswamy Iyer with his family settled near the Kaveri delta in a place named Aduthurai.

Krishnamurthi was the fourth son and the youngest. His three elder brothers studied Sanskrit and were teachers in the *patashala*. With the added income, life was more comfortable. Sri Ramaswamay Iyer wanted his youngest son Krishnamurthi to study English so that he could have better prospects. Krishnmurthi was sent to a mission school in Tiruvidaimaruthur.

Krishnamurthi proved to be a diligent student and was liked by his teachers. From here he went to a better school in Kumbakonam and then he was sent to Trivandrum where the standard of education was high. At 19 he passed his matriculation examination.

Krishnamurthi was keen to study Sanskrit so he learnt Sanskrit under Bala Saraswathi Battar Sri Narayana Sastrigal and became proficient in the knowledge of the Vedas and Upanishads. Having mastered Sanskrit he was keen to study Tamil, his mother tongue. He had a great love for Tamil and learnt the *Tevaram, Tiruvachakam* and the Vaishnavite texts *Nalayira Divyaprabandham.*

He now took up a job in the settlement office in Salem (a district 200 miles from Chennai) on a monthly salary of Rs. 50. A hundred years ago this was a princely salary. But Krishanmurthi was not elated by his achievments. His mind was always engaged in meditating on God. He performed his office duties efficiently, but whenever he had some leisure, he would sit in his chair in deep meditation. His bosses respected him for his work and for his devotion to God and increased his salary to Rs. 60.

Now the events that were written about at the beginning of this narrative took place.

Krishnamurthi gave his passbook with the savings of Rs. 500 to his father and brother and with only the clothes he was wearing walked out of their lives, out of the bonds of a family life, to pursue a path, which was close to his heart — renunciation and surrender to God.

Krishnamurthi made the hazardous journey to Varanasi (Kashi) in search of a *guru*. He reached Varansi and worshipped at the temples of Visalakshi, Annapurni and Lord Vishwanath. He prayed earnestly that he should find a *guru* under whom he could gain spiritual knowledge. He found his *guru* in Tiruvannamalai Dakshinamurthy Swamigal, who in turn was a disciple of Mannarkudi Raju Shastrigal.

Krishnamurthi acquired *Brahma-jnana*, meaning the supreme knowledge, from his *guru*. Subsequently he spent six months with a Mauna Swami who by his silence initiated him into the essence of self-realization. He was now ready to take *sannyasa*, but was troubled by the thought that the Shastras enjoined a life of a householder on the *sadhaka* and the performing of dharmic duties expounded by the Shastras before taking Sanyas. But his *guru* Dakshinamurthy Swamigal dispelled his doubts and gave instances of *brahmacharis* taking *sannyasa* beginning with Adi Shankara who was a mere boy when he made his mother give him permission to take *sannyasa* which is a story in itself. Acting according to his *guru*'s instruction, he wrote to his parents seeking their permission to take *sannyasa*. Very soon he had a letter from his father in reply to his request. It was that Krishnamurthi should return immediately and should not take *sannyasa*.

With his *guru*'s blessings Krishnamurthi set out for his village. The day he reached the village he got the news that his father had died in the early hours that very morning, and the body had been taken to the cremation grounds. Without going home he went straight there. His brothers and other relatives asked him to join the rituals being performed for the cremation, but he refused and stood at a distance. His relatives abused him and cursed him, but he remained silent. Among those present was one man who, recognizing his divinity, spoke up for Krishnamurthi. He told those assembled, "his father will go to heaven because of this son of his, who is a saint. Leave him alone." Krishnamurthi did not go home.

After the thirteen days rituals were over, his brothers went to Puducottai where they were earning their livlihood. Krishnamurthi also went to Puducottai but he did not go home. He begged for his food from the households in the Aghraharam as behoves renunciates observing the practice of *madhukari*. He took six handfulls of food for himself and with the rest he fed the crows. He was still waiting for God to show him the path to attain liberation.

At that time in the city of Madurai there was a saint who was known by two names — one was Judge Swamigal, the other was Sadashiva Brahmendrar (not to be confused with the Nerur Saint). This saint also was an *avadhuta* (a naked saint). Krishnamurthi came to hear of this saint. As he was eager to get initiation into sanyas by a *guru*, he at once went to Madurai to see the Swamigal. The Swamigal, when he saw Krishnamurthi, was convinced that he had the qualities which made him fit to be initiated into *sannyasa*. He, however, advised him to get the consent of his parents. Krishnamurthi replied that he had only his mother. The Swamigal told him to get the permission of his mother who had brought him into this world and whose loving hands had fed him.

What could he do? He went to Kanapatti a place only a few miles from Madurai where his mother was living. Krishnamurthi went to his mother and with only a small piece of cloth around him went round her three times, and sat down beside her. He explained to her his mental state and his spiritual development and his desire to take *sannyasa*. It can be taken that he convinced her and got her consent because while he was there, even that small piece of cloth he was wearing fell from his body. His brothers who were standing near were stunned by this and looked with awe at their younger brother.

Krishnamurthi stood up and with folded hands bid good bye to all of them forever and left the place — the date was 23 June 1899. He was now roaming the streets of Tirukkovilur, a young handsome 28 year old man stark naked, an *avadhuta* heedless of the abuses and stones hurled at him.

There were some brahmins who wanted to teach him a lesson. They forcibly made him sit and had his moustache and flowing beard cut and poured water on his head. They pulled him and dragged him around the village. But Krishnamurthi was absolutely unconcerned and allowed himself to be ill-treated without protesting. Maybe if he had shown anger they might have been more cruel. After some days when they saw that this man could not be provoked, they felt ashamed and stopped their teasing. They even asked for his forgiveness.

In the district of Tiruchirapalli there lived a very rich man named Sri Thandava Raya Pillai. He had built a temple for Lord Thandava, the youngest of the two sons of Lord Shiv, also known as Murugan and Subrahmanya. For the laying of the foundation stone for the temple, His Holiness Jagadguru Sringeri Sri Sachidananda Narasimha Bharati Swamigal had come. Similarly when the temple was completed he had come for the *kumbhabhishekham* or consecration ceremony.

This Thandavaraya Pillai who was a great Shiva devotee wanted to test the young *avadhuta* Swami and arranged for some beautiful prostitutes to visit him. However, for this Swami it did not matter who came to visit him because he was totally unaware of their presence. It was the women themselves who were ashamed of themselves and prostrating before him with devotion, went away.

Once, during his wanderings he came to Nerur, the *samadhi* of Sri Sadashiva Brahmendra, the *mauni* (silent) saint and composer of many devotional songs in Sanskrit. Krishnamurthi (henceforth to be referred to as Swamigal) spent some days in meditation there. From there he travelled the length and breadth of Cholamandalam on foot and came to Tiruvannamalai where Bhagavan Ramana Maharishi's Ashram was.

But Swamigal could not be peaceful there as many of his relatives, hearing of his advent there, came to Tiruvannamalai and began pestering him. So Swamigal quietly left that place and went to Kottimalai. On his way he had to pass through Salem town. Seeing a naked Swami people threw stones and beat him up and the police arrested the Swami instead of reprimanding his tormentors. Krishnaswamy Iyer, a leading advocate of Salem, came to know of this and argued the Swamigal's case in court. He was able to convince the court that a state of avadhuta was recognized and accepted in Hindu Shastras as a form of renunciation which only great saints could undertake. The Swamigal was released and Krishnaswamy Iyer took him to his house.

Swamigal throughout remained smiling and unconcerned even when he was in jail and when he was taken to the lawyer's house. It was while he was at the lawyer's house that people came to recognize his greatness. People thronged to seek his blessings. Many came with problems of health and were cured by Swamigal's *vibhuti prasada.* Many spiritual aspirants became his disciples.

The Swamigal did not tarry long in Salem. He set out on foot to a place called Senthamangalam. The road to Senthamangalam went winding like a snake between hills. There were rivers and waterfalls. Tall trees grew thickly on the hills making the place cool and enchanting to behold. Like the caves in the mountain of Arunachala in Tiruvannamalai, here too there were caves hidden among the rocks. It was an ideal setting for a recluse or a sannyasi to meditate.

Senthamangalam was a charming village with a small Shiva temple in the agraharam. In the town, Muslim weavers lived in large numbers. Our *avadhuta* Swamigal walked through the Muslim occupied area in his state of physical nakedness and semi-consciousness. This angered the Muslims who thought this was a deliberate act of the Hindus to insult them and they tied the Swamigal to a pillar and beat him. Seeing this a woman who belonged to the Rudra Kanikaiyar (*devadasi* caste who were temple dancers) named Shivabhagyam explained to the Muslims that the Swamigal was a saint and was a self-realized soul. He was neither aware of where he was going nor was he aware of the people around him. She took him to her house and kept him there for some days and served him with devotion. Swamigal went on his wanderings. If anyone gave him food he would eat but otherwise he went without food.

The Swamigal's greatness and divinity attracted a few learned men to become his devotees. Among them there were a retired judge named Sundara Chettiar and Union Chairman Ramaswamy Chettiar. They consulted with each other and came to a decision. They wanted him to reside in Sannyasi Karadu which was a hill with rocks and a cave with a rivulet flowing where he could stay without being troubled by unwanted attention. But they could not persuade the Swamigal to move there. Perhaps he knew he had to undergo more trials and tribulations, even character assassination and calumny, before he could live in peace and solitude. Soon after this, it was reported that a young girl had disappeared from Kollimalai and the hill tribals suspected the *avadhuta* Swamigal and began to abuse him and ill-treat him. A Revenue inspector of that area came to know of this and rescued the Swamigal from Kollimalai and brought him to his house.

The Swami's body bore wounds from the beating and the inspector applied ointments and with great devotion attended on him. But when his physical condition improved, Swamigal was again restless and went into the forest roaming and experiencing bliss in solitude. He would sometimes go into a cave and go into deep samadhi for days oblivious to the world.

Some of Swamigal's disciples in Senthamangalam worried about his deteriorating health. They went in search of him and literally begged him to allow them to take him to a safer place and eventually, they succeeded in bringing him to Sannyasi Karadu, a much more secluded place. The rich merchants of Senthamangalam put up a porch in front of the cave, where devotees could sit and have *darshana* of the Swamigal. The cave was fitted with a door. The Swamigal went inside and asked them to lock it on the outside and never open it without his permission. Seven months went by and the cave remained locked.

The Collector of Senthamangalam came to know of this and declared that locking up a man inside was against the law. He ordered the door to be opened. They found the

Swamigal lying flat on his back as if dead. They gently carried him out of the cave and found his body warm and fresh. But it seemed a lifeless body. So the Collector ordered his assistants to throw the body down the hill and went away. But before that could be done, Swamigal awoke from his deep *samadhi* and sat up. Immediately the Collector was informed and he felt very repentant that he had harshly ordered a live person to be thrown away down the hill, not knowing that he was a saint. He came running to the Swamigal, fell at his feet and asked for his forgiveness. From now on, Swamigal came to be known as Senthamangalam Sri Swayam Prakasa Swamigal.

The period was early twentieth century. The colonial influence was changing the lives of many people. English education brought in Western ideas. The traditional ritualistic way of life was slowly giving way to progressive ideas and young people adopted the Western dress of trousers or pants as it is now called. In short, India was in a state of transition.

Swamigal felt that he should travel to all corners of Bharata Desham and try to impart spiritual knowledge to those who sought it, and bless the suffering humanity by his divine healing touch. During his travels Swamigal performed many miracles. It is not possible to write a detailed account of all the wonderful miracles that took place in this short biography but a few are included here. Like a guiding light he changed the lives of many people bringing in them spiritual transformation.

In the course of his travels he came to Tiruchirapalli. At one point the River Kaveri had to be crossed to reach the other side. The boatman who plied passengers across refused to take the *avadhuta* Swamigal in his boat. Swamigal calmly threw his palm leaf fan into the water and stepping on it crossed the river to the amazement of the spectators.

Another such incident took place in Tiruchi. Some mischievous young men brought a boy (who was pretending to be dead) wrapped up in a cloth like a shroud and wanting to test Swamigal's powers put the boy in front of him and asked him to bring the dead boy to life. Swamigal said "Oh, is that so? Poor boy" and went on his way. But when the boy's friends laughingly asked the boy to get up they found that he was indeed dead. They ran after Swamigal, fell at his feet and pleaded with him to bring the boy to life, but the Swamigal only said, "that is his fate."

It is recorded that Swamigal went to Aduthurai and there in the temple *dwarasthambham* (pillar in the centre of the quadrangle) with his legs twined around the pillar and head down, went into samadhi for four days.

Once it happened that some people with evil intentions gave him milk mixed with milk from the poisonous cactus. Swamigal drank the poisoned milk which had no effect on him.

In this manner, performing many miracles, Swamigal reached the Himalayas and arrived at Badarikaashram (Badrinath). Swamigal stayed there for several years in *tapas*. One day Lord Dattatreya appeared before him and told him that in the south no one knew about him, so he wanted Swamigal to build a temple for him in the south and propagate the worship of Dattatreya. Swayam Prakasa Swamigal blessed by the vision of the Lord, returned to Senthamangalam after an absence of seventeen years.

According to Lord Dattatreya's command, Swamigal collected funds and built a temple for the Lord and performed the *kumbhabhishekham*. The place now is called Dattagiri in Senthamangalam district. Swamigal spent his days in the Sannyasi Karadu cave. He initiated many disciples into *sannyasa,* prominent among whom were Nijananda, Shivananda and Abhayananda. Because of the efforts of these three disciples, the temple was built in a short time. Even now, every year Datta Jayanti is celebrated with great pomp in this temple. Other disciples of Swamigal were Shankarananda who undertook the building of the *athishthanam* for his *guru*. Swami Thuriyananda has published a book of questions and answers titled *Prashnotamalika,* a compilation of questions asked by devotees and answered by Swamigal. Krishnananda, another *sannyasi* disciple of Swayam Prakasa Swamigal, travelled to Badrinath on foot and eventually settled in an *ashram* in Visalur, a village in Kumbakonam. Sri Shanthananda Swamigal has established a Bhuvaneshwari Peetham in Puducottai. Another great devotee and disciple of Swamigal, Sri Sukhananda with the blessings and encouragement of his *guru,* brought out a book on the life of Swamigal written by Dindigul Gurupadasekharan.

Thus the great Avadhuta Sri Swayam Prakasa Swamigal not only attained godliness himself but also showed the path to attain self-realization and renunciation to many spiritual aspirants. The saint born in the year 1871 attained the feet of the Lord on 29 December 1948.

12

Andavan Pichhai Amma

MARAGATHAVALLI was only three years old when she lost her mother. As her father, Sri Shankara Narayana Shastri, married a second time, she was brought up by her paternal grandmother Sundari. Maragathavalli was a shy child and did not play with the other children. Her speech was slow and impaired, and so she remained quiet most of the time. She was called dumb and dim-witted and teased by everyone.

Her maternal grandfather on his deathbed had made his friend and distant cousin, Mylapore Guruswamy Shastri promise him that he would take care of his motherless granddaughter and get her married to his second son Narasimhan. Narasimhan who was studying for the bar was not agreeable to marrying a girl so much younger than him. His mother was also not in favour of this alliance, but Guruswamy overruled them all and fulfilled his promise to his friend. The wedding took place in April 1908. Maragathavalli was nine years old and Narasimhan was twenty. Her dowry consisted of two bungalows, some vessels and enough jewellery to adorn her from head to foot. She stayed for a while with her in-laws. In September, during the *Navaratri* celebrations, she went to her father's house.

One day, Maragathavalli, who was ten years old at that time, went into her father's library. She stood boldly by his side. Her father, who was at work, was surprised. She had never before approached him for anything nor even spoken

7. Andavan Pichchai Amma.

to him. "What do you want child?" he asked, as he beckoned her to come close to him. She put her arms around him and wept bitterly. With love and concern, her father sat her on his lap. He consoled her, and asked, "why are you crying my child? Did anyone scold you? Are you unwell?" The little girl put her hand to her heart and asked, "shall I tell you what is happening here?" "Certainly tell me about what is troubling you," her father reassuringly, said.

Maragatham stood up, wiped her tears and folding her palms together as in prayer, sang in a loud and melodious voice a poem of three stanzas in the Raga Mohanam. The poem was so beautiful and had such a depth of meaning that her father Shankara Narayana Shastri was astounded. "Who taught you this song?" he asked her. His daughter replied, "no one taught me, it just came to me. I have wanted to tell you something since yesterday." "What happened yesterday?" her father asked her. "Yesterday, Tiruthanikai Murugan came on His peacock, asked me to put out my tongue, and with his *Vel* (spear) wrote something on it. I immediately started singing. I sang for Murugan. Would you like to hear that song?" She sang a song on Lord Muruga of Tiruthani. "Father, when I sang this song, Murugan told me, "my child, I will always be with you. Now you will speak, sing and study like other children," and He placed His hand on my head and said, *om saravanabhava, shanmugam tharakam*," and disappeared. Her father looked as if he did not believe her and asked her to sing on her own parents, as the Shastras say, "one's mother and father are the first Gods." Maragatham sang and the song contained the names "Pon" meaning Lakshmi, her mother's name, and "Maal," meaning Narayanan, her father's name. Again her father wanted to test her and said, "Now that you are married, your husband is everything to you, more than your parents, more than God. Therefore sing a poem on your husband." Maragatham sang a beautiful song on her husband extolling the virtues of a chaste wife, singing "so will I be to my husband Narahari (Narasimhan)."

Her father was overjoyed and carrying her, ran to the puja room where his elder brother Venkatasubbier was praying and shouted, "Anna, Anna see, this child is singing so beautifully. I who am not easily moved have been shaken by this miracle. We thought this daughter of mine was dumb and dull-witted. Now I see she is Parashakti herself." His eyes were flowing with tears. Her grandmother Sundari who loved her very much and was saddened by the fact that she was not normal like the other children was now very happy, and hugged her granddaughter with joy and blessed her. After this incident, Maragatham was very good in whatever she did.

Thandalam Shankara Narayana Shastri, father of Maragatham, was an erudite scholar, well versed in the knowledge of the Vedas and Upanishads. He was also proficient in English, Tamil and Sanskrit, and had written books in these languages. By profession he was a lawyer and had a very lucrative practice. He was a painter and had painted pictures of Nataraja (*tandava-rahasyam*), Raja Rajeshwari, Gayatri and other deities. He was a *jnani* and a Vedantin. He was always to be found in his large library room, either reading or meditating. His wife was Sitalakshmi. Her first child, a boy, was named Sreenivasan. In 1899 a daughter was born. She was called Maragathavalli. The naming of this child also has a special significance attached to it. Her uncle Venkatasubbier had won a difficult case in court and his client, a *zamindar*, apart from paying him a hefty fee, also presented him in gratitude with a jade (Maragatha) idol of Devi. This was installed in the *puja* room and that same evening

Sitalakshmi delivered a girl. The baby girl was therefore named Maragathavalli. When Maragathavalli was one and a half years old, Sitalakshmi gave birth to a son Subrahmanyam and eighteen months later she died.

Shankara Narayana Sastri married again. His wife was too young to take care of the three motherless children, so Sundari *paatti* (their paternal grandmother) brought them up. His second wife Rajamma had three boys and a girl. But Shastri had no time for his wife or for his children since he spent the major part of his time studying and meditating.

His elder brother Venkatasubbier was also a leading lawyer and specialized in criminal cases (the younger brother took up civil cases). Venkatasubbier had only one daughter and later legally adopted Subrahmaniam, Maragatham's younger brother.

Maragatham's paternal grandfather was Thandalam Ramakrishna Shastri. He studied the Vedas and Upanishads under one Ishwara Jata Vallabha, a learned *pundit*. Ramakrishna Shastri became so proficient in expounding the Vedas that he was given the title, "Veda Nipuna." He did not want to marry and was a bachelor till he was forty, but his *guru* persuaded him to marry his own daughter Sundari who was only ten.

The couple were very well off with extensive properties at a place called Santhana Cheri on the banks of the Palar river opposite Athur in Chingleput district. In course of time Sundari gave birth to two sons and two daughters. Once during a flood Shastri picked up a box floating in the swollen waters of the river which contained *vigrahams* of Lord Venkateshwara, Sridevi and Bhudevi and many *saligramams* (symbolic representation of Vishnu) besides. These have ever since remained with the family.

Once as Shastri was giving a discourse on *Skanda Puranam* with his younger son Shankara Narayanan fanning him, he stopped in the middle of a sentence and uttering the words, "Hara, Hara Subrahmaniam" gave up his *prana*. Sundari brought up her children well and both sons became lawyers.

It was to this illustrious lineage that Maragatham belonged. Her marriage took place at the tender age of nine to a man eleven years older. Narasimhan who was preparing for the legal profession, reluctantly accepted his child bride.

Maragatham went to live in her husband's house. It was a large household, her husband's elder brother Subrahmaniam was there with his wife and five children — two boys and three girls. This brother was a liability as he was not an earning member. One of her sisters-in-law who was no more, had left a daughter to be brought up by her brother. She and Maragatham were of the same age and became friends. Her youngest sister-in-law, her husband and family of two boys and three girls were also part of the household. Maragatham's father-in-law had retired and the family had migrated to Madras. He built a large house in Mylapore.

Her husband was studying for law and did not care to look at her or talk to her. His father made great efforts to make his son soften towards his wife. Her mother-in-law got over her disappointment and tried to treat her with sympathy but could not understand and forgive her being so different from other girls of her age.

Narasimhan passed his law examination with flying colours and started practice in the courts. One by one those who loved Maragatham passed away. Her grandmother Sundari paatti, her uncle Venkatasubbier, and her father-in-law Guruswamy Shastri died in quick succession. Maragatham felt their loss very keenly and felt she was now all alone without any moral support.

It was only three years since she came to live with her husband and she had not yet conceived, but her mother-in-law and others were already talking of her as a barren woman. They attempted to arrange a second marriage for Narasimhan. Maragatham was so miserable and scared that she offered her gold chain threaded with gold sovereigns to Lord Murugan of Tiruthani if he would save her from the fate of an abandoned wife.

Maragatham's first child born in 1912 was stillborn when she herself was only thirteen. There were complications during the delivery and the doctor pronounced that she was not likely to have any more children. Again the talk of a second marriage for Narasimhan was considered; but Narasimhan was firm in his resolve, "children or no children," he said, "I will not marry a second time." By God's grace five years later in 1917 Maragatham gave birth to a healthy boy who was named Guruswamy after his paternal grandfather.

Maragatham's father loved this grandson of his very much. When the child was ten months old, her father fell seriously ill and expressed a wish to see his daughter and grandson. Maragatham was not aware of the seriousness of his condition. She stayed overnight. Next morning when the first rays of the sun streamed through his window, he gazed at the sun and told his daughter that the sun who derived his light from the source that lay at the substratum of all creation, Lord Narayana, could be seen even with the naked eye. He repeated the Gayatri *mantra* asking Maragatham to repeat it after him; smiling and with eyes wide open, he left his mortal coil.

As all these events were happening Maragatham never for a moment forgot her Murugan and his dazzling vision.

She held Him in her heart, and performed her duties as wife, daughter-in-law and mother.

This state of affairs changed during her fifth delivery. Maragatham had not been keeping well this time. Just two days before Skanda Shashti which in that year 1924 fell in October, she got up early to have a bath but even before she could bathe she developed labour pains and the baby, a son, was born without even the doctor or midwife attending. The child was named Seshadri.

On every Skanda Shashti day it was the practice of the family to offer Rs. 50 to the nearby Subrahmanya temple. The *pujari* who came to collect the money gave the news that the person who offered to donate Rs. 250 for the *Puja* had suddenly expired the previous day. Maragatham's mother-in-law was happy that a boy was born on the eve of Skanda Shashti and that too without any doctor's expense for which she would have had to pay Rs. 250. So she generously offered to undertake the expense of the *puja* and paid the *pujari* Rs. 250.

On the *Shashti* night, the procession from the temple came to their house and the *Sura Samhara* festival in which the demon Surapadma is killed by Murugan, was celebrated with fireworks there. Everyone except Maragatham, who was confined to her room, watched the festivities which lasted until midnight. Even though the delivery was easy and quick with not even time to call the doctor, Maragatham was very weak and was having high fever. On Skanda Shashti day she was tossing about with fever not knowing whether she was dreaming or awake, she had a vision of Lord Muruga. She saw a garden and in the centre there was a small *samadhi* type temple. It was full moon day and the place was bathed in moonlight. She went round the temple and saw a small lighted lamp inside and the figure of Bala Murugan about a foot tall.

Lost in devotion she made obeisance. Suddenly she saw Him, a curly haired boy, with large, enchanting eyes, coming towards her, the anklets on His feet jingling, and in His hand a golden *Vel*, He appealed to Maragathammal to lift him. He put His arms around her and laughed a musical laugh like the tinkling of bells. "You are my mother, sing a lullaby for me," He said. Maragatham stood dazed and the Lord disappeared. She forgot her sick body, she forgot the world and fell down like a rootless tree.

The newborn baby was crying lustily and she regained consciousness. The whole night the joy of seeing the Lord in her vision and the sorrow at His separation kept her awake. Towards morning she must have dozed off when a flood of devotional songs flowed from her, disturbing her sleep. There were more than 200 songs in different musical metres — Andadi, Venba, Ahaval and Viruttam, all came pouring out. As she was very weak after the delivery, her brother-in-law's daughter had stayed with her. She asked her to write down the songs as she sang. In the morning she told her mother-in-law whom she considered her mother about her vision and showed her the sheaf of songs written down.

Her mother-in-law did daily *puja* and observed fasts on Ekadashi and other important days, and seemed to be a religious person, but she reacted with unexpected harshness to Maragatham's narration of her unique spiritual experience. After listening to her daughter-in-law she said, "Enough of your prattle. If you sing in praise of that aandi (beggar) the whole family will go abegging. For those who are householders and live in a family this kind of behaviour is not correct. If you sing poems, penury will hit us. No poet is rich. You do not know about these things. If one does Lakshmi *puja* everyday, lighting the lamp, that is enough for a householder. Forget about singing poems. Live happily with your husband and your children. In future if songs come to you do not put them down in writing." She then collected all the 200 songs Maragatham had proudly shown her and locked them up in her trunk. She also extracted a promise from her daughter-in-law and made her swear by her children, her husband and Murugan, that she would not compose or sing songs in future.

Maragatham was heartbroken. That which even seers and *yogis* do penance to obtain, had come to her easily; Murugan came to her, she had lifted Bala Murugan and sang for him. Now her mother-in-law has ordained that she should not even utter His name aloud. What a sinner she was, she thought, and cried silently lest her mother-in-law abuse her for displaying her sorrow. "O! Muruga you came to me when I was ten years old, now after fourteen years you again came to me, my Lord Muruga. You made me sing — it is a miracle I could never forget. My Muruga, because of this promise extracted from me, please do not come before me, but dwell in my heart, and never show yourself to me lest it bring forth my devotion in the form of songs which I am forbidden to sing or write." Thus from the year 1924 to 1948 Maragatham kept her Murugan, her Shanmuga, her Kandan, within her body, carrying Him like a child in the womb. Recording this incident years later, she wrote a poem in Tamil which defies translation. After twenty-four years of being imprisoned in her heart the Lord Himself ended his exile and came to Maragatham-who later on came to be known as Andavan Pichhai Amma — again.

Maragathavalli bore ten children. The first was a boy who was stillborn. One girl Padma was an extraordinary child. She was sick with an enlarged liver and spleen, but she appeared to be a divine child. She used to weave flower garlands and take them to the nearby Devi temple. Slowly her eyes got weaker and weaker and she became blind. Once, the Kanchi Paramacharya had come on a visit to Madras. Amma took her daughter along with her to see him; Paramacharyal recommended an eye specialist. As it was Monday, the sage was observing *mauna vratam* (vow of silence). So he wrote down the instructions. Acharyal blessed the child and indicated that she would regain her eye sight but that her life would be very short. The specialist recommended by Acharyal treated her and Padma regained her sight.

One evening in 1936 she suffered a severe pain in the abdomen and died with the flower garland in her hand. Strangely, the *pujari* in the temple saw the child bringing the flower garland as usual. He asked her not to enter the *sanctum sanctorum* as it was lighting time, but Padma took no heed of his words and went straight into the *garbha-griha* never to return. He came to know later about the death of the child which had taken place a little earlier. The divine child was absorbed in Devi. Padma was seven years old when she died.

Amma's mother-in-law Kaveriamma was bedridden for six long years and had to be nursed. She wanted only Amma to nurse her. She passed away in 1930, the year Kalpagam, Amma's daughter was married. In 1936 Amma's last and youngest son Vasudevan was born. Of the nine children born to her — six sons and three daughters — one daughter Padma died and also two sons. One of them, Shankaran who after an accident in childhood was mentally retarded, suffered very much and died at the age of 21. The youngest son Vasudevan died of a serious illness when he was a child.

Since his own family was growing in size, Narasimhan requested his brother and family to live separately. He got his brother's three daughters married off, spending for the dowry, jewels and for the marriage arrangements. He also requested his sister and family to live separately, but continued to support them with funds. The rest of Amma's children did very well. Guruswamy and Ganapathy were doctors. Seshadri passed his MA in mathematics with a First division and Venkataraman qualified as an engineer. Her two daughters Kalpagam and Kamakshi were also well married. Kalpagam was in Madras and Kamakshi was in Delhi. Amma, although she loved her family and served them well, was not affected by the sorrows or joys that occurred in her life. Ever since her promise to her mother-in-law she had no vision of the Lord nor did songs come to her. Murugan was within her constantly and her mind was turned within (*antarmukha*).

A great turning point in Amma's life came in the year 1948. In March that year Narasimhan celebrated his 60th birthday. Many relations had come for the function. After it was over, Amma and three other ladies decided to go to Sri Sailam. All of them went late in the evening to the Patala Ganga, bathed and filled their pitchers with water for performing *abhishekam* to Lord Mallikarjuna. It was a steep climb to the top of the hill and it was dark. They had heard that there were wild animals roaming in the dark. Suddenly a well-built man, past middle age, was coming towards them. He took Amma's pitcher from her and told them that he would escort them to the top. When they reached the top, the stranger handed Amma's pitcher to her and disappeared.

That night when they were all sleeping, Amma, at 3 O' clock in the morning, had a dream. The same person who had helped them on the hill, appeared before her and gave her the *shadakshari mantra* (the *bija mantra* for Murugan), and told her that he would meet her again on the next *Shivaratri* day. He also told her that her life would end on *Vaishakhi Purnima* the same year (1948).

It was *Vaishakhi Purnima* and Amma was very ill after a fall from the staircase. The doctors diagnosed it as a severe heart attack. Her two doctor sons were also present. Slowly the pulse grew very feeble and they thought the end had come and her children started wailing but after awhile the heart beat feebly revived, grew stronger and Amma survived.

But not as Maragathavalli — that soul had left this body, and another soul had entered it.

In Pinnavasal, a place near Tiruchi, a disciple of Sadashiva Brahmendrar — named Ramakrishna or Pinnavasal Swami as he came to be called — attained *mahasamadhi* in 1943. Swami had told his devotees that after his passing away they should not close the brick *samadhi* (built over his body) completely but leave a space so that his spirit could come out when it wanted to.

This Ramakrishna who was a disciple and ardent devotee of Sadashiva Brahmendrar, was a married man. When he decided to take to the path of renunciation, his wife who was devoted to him pleaded with him to allow her to be with him and serve him, not as a wife but as a devotee. But Ramakrishna rudely drove her away. That helpless lady who had been spurned, cursed her husband to be born a woman in order to experience the sufferings of a woman. Being a true *pativrata* (chaste woman) her curse would have given Ramakrishna another birth in a womb. Therefore his Guru Sadashiva Brahmendrar (who had attained *samadhi*, only recently) spoke to him in a vision at the precise moment Maragatham was dying. He told him, "Go, enter the body of this saint whose body was a temple in which Lord Muruga resided, and avoid the suffering of taking birth again in a womb."

Thus the turning point in Andavan Pichhai's life came when she outwardly had a woman's body but since a man had entered it, she had a man's physical urges. This dual existence caused her great physical suffering.

When Amma regained consciousness, she did not recognize her own family. She/He was confused. "Who is this mother they are referring to? Who am I? Is this body a woman to be called mother? If so, who is the one inside?" After these thoughts she again closed her eyes in exhaustion. Amma was bedridden for nearly six months. She still did not recognize her own children. Everyone was worried at this strange reaction and behaviour of Amma.

One day she heard a voice saying "time will reveal what the soul hankers after. What you asked for you have obtained. You had asked for an abode where you could live peacefully. This body has been the temple of the Lord for 24 years, worshipped with incessant prayer. You have avoided the miseries of a mother's womb. You will visit many *kshetra*s (sacred places) and have *darshana* of great saints. Take on the duties that come before you and surrender yourself unto the Lord." Hearing this, Amma realized the truth in a flash and fell down from the cot crying, "O! Lord." Her family came rushing to her and thought that she had suffered another setback, but in truth Amma felt at peace. She now knew who she was, and she recognized the fact that a man's soul had entered her body. She accepted this as a divine dispensation.

From now on, Andavan Pichhai as Amma came to be called for nearly 40 years travelled the length and breadth of Bharat, from the extreme south to Badrinath in the Himalayas in the north. She had the *darshana* of many saints, and her life took on an entirely different turn.

Amma's health was not good; she had not regained strength and was very weak. One day a cousin Balambika came to see her. She wanted Amma to write a special poem for a women's magazine *Kumkumam*. After Amma's mother-in-law passed away, her steel trunk in which she had kept Amma's songs was opened. To the utter amazement of everyone, all the notebooks and other papers in which her songs were written were intact and in good condition, but the fat wad of bank notes her mother-in-law had kept in a cardboard box was all eaten up by termites and had to be thrown away.

When Balambika asked her for a poem, Amma gave the whole song collection to her and told her, "Do what you like with it." The bundle contained among other poems *Thanikesan Andhadi, Murugan Pancharatnam, Mayil Paththu* (ten stanzas on the peacock), *Seval Paththu* (ten songs on the greatness of the cock which is found at Murugan's side), and *Vel Paththu* (ten songs on the spear which Murugan holds).

For 24 years Amma did not have a vision of Lord Murugan. She had kept Him inside her. On 21 January 1949 Lord Murugan appeared to Amma in the night. He was wearing ochre robes, there was a *rudraksha mala* round His neck and on His arms. As always He had His Vel. Lord Muruga came near Amma, lifted up her face with His divine hands and said, "Don't you know me?" Amma cried aloud, "Muruga, Muruga," and fell at His feet. "Yesterday you gave away all my songs. Do you not like them or need them anymore? From today you are going to sing and adorn me with garlands of your songs (called Paamaalai in Tamizh). More than garlands of gold, beads and flowers, I like garlands of songs sung with devotion. So start singing as you used to before," said the Lord. "O Lord!," cried Amma, "The soul that was in this body has fled. Don't you know who I am now? Why do you tease me?" The Lord smiled and said "Yes, the nightingale that was in this body has fled. True, I also know who you are now. Are you the one who is singing? I am the doer, I make you sing. Life is full of joys and sorrows, be a witness to all that is to happen henceforth," and the Lord disappeared in a brilliant flash of light. Amma then crying aloud "Muruga" lost her sense of identity and out of her, at His behest, came exquisite compositions. The first of these was "Arunodaya" which was a complete description of her dazzling vision of Murugan.

Amma moved to her daughter Kalpagam's house in Mylapore. It took nearly eight months for her to regain normal health. A day prior to *Shivaratri*, Kalpagam showed Amma a newspaper photo of Tirupugazh Mani. Amma was surprised to see that this was the person who had helped them in Sri Sailam, and in her dream had told her he would meet her on the next *Shivaratri*. He had also predicted her end on *Vaishakhi Purnima* day and that had happened. Amma expressed a desire to see this person and although she was ill she went with Kalpagam to his house. When they reached his house, Tirupugazh Mani was just then leaving and asked them to come the next day.

Amma placed the fruits she had brought for him at his feet and also a poem on him as her *guru*. She also told him how he had helped her in Sri Sailam and initiated her with the *shadakshara mantra*. He was taken aback as he had never been to Sri Sailam at all, "all this is God's doing," he said. Next day Tirupugazh Mani himself went to see Amma. It seems the previous night he had a dream and he saw his *guru* Pinnavasal Swami telling him, "I came to you and you did not recognize me." Just before his *samadhi* Pinnavasal Swami had promised Tirupugazh Mani — who was his disciple — that he would give him *darshana* in some other form. Tirupugazh Mani had answered that he would recognize him in any form. But the previous morning when Amma came he not only did not recognise him but asked Amma to come the next day. He asked his secretary Balambika if she knew Amma. Balambika said she is Andavan Pichhai whose songs he himself was publishing. And that was how he came to Amma's house. Amma placed all that she had written in a sandalwood box and gave it away to Tirupugazh Mani.

Another miraculous event happened to Amma in Delhi in the year 1973, when she was staying with her daughter Kamakshi. One day, Amma, unable to sleep, was sitting up, with her grandchildren sleeping near her. The room was dimly lit by a small lamp. Suddenly there was a bright light which spread and lighted up the room. She saw Lord Ganesha wearing a yellow garment with a flower garland round his neck. He lifted his trunk and tapped her on the head and pointed up. Amma witnessed an incredible scene, the rotating of a wheel of light. As she watched it with amazement, the speed slowed down and in the centre on a golden seat there was a long Vel. From underneath the wheel the sacred emblems of Muruga, the Cock and Peacock were looking at the Vel. The wheel turned into *om* and Lord Muruga with his hands on the peacock's neck — the same form of Muruga who had appeared to her after 24 years (when he had appeared on 21 January 1949) — was smiling and with eyes dancing in joy kept plucking the feathers from the peacock and was throwing them on Amma. Suddenly it became dark and the scene disappeared. Next day she asked her daughter Kalpagam who could draw and paint, to depict the scene she described on a canvas. As if to prove that it was not a dream, the room was strewn with peacock feathers. Amma was in total bliss for some time and wrote a garland of a hundred and eight songs on the vision and called it Arulvilakka Malai.

Amma (who was now aware of herself as Pinnavasal Swami) as foretold by Lord Muruga, had the opportunity to visit many temples and also have the *darshana* of great *gurus* and saints. Narasimhan also accompanied her. Once when

Amma and her husband went to Kancheepuram, the Kanchi Paramacharya changed the nomenclature Pichhi meaning "mad" which Amma had given herself, to "Andavan Pichhai" — "gift of God."

In March 1950 Amma went with a party to Tiruvannamalai. By the time they reached the temple it was late in the night and the *pujari* was locking the doors. Half the party went away but Amma and the rest stayed back. They told the *pujari* they would like to worship Arunachaleshwara at least through the grills. When they went near the Devi shrine they saw a charming young lad sitting on the steps and singing in a melodious voice. He told them that he would perform archana to the Devi for them. The party said that they had not brought any flowers, fruits or coconuts for the *puja*. The boy replied that there was a plate full of all these required items inside the sanctum, and he would do the *puja* from that. The boy then opened the door of the sanctum and did the *puja* and *archana* reciting the *mantra*s and gave them *prasada*. They all had a good *darshana* of Devi. No one had any money with them, only Amma had a ring-like copper coin (quarter *anna*) and gave him that. The boy took it and wore it on his little finger and said he would take his full *dakshina* the next day. They asked him his name and the boy replied it was Dandapani. While Amma and the others were coming out the lights went out. Everyone rushed out except Amma. The boy Dandapani caught hold of her hand and led her to a place where there was a small image of Murugan. It was at that spot that Murugan had emerged form a pillar to give *darshana* to Arunagirinathar, the saint and composer of the Tirupugazh. Dandapani told Amma that he always stayed in that temple, and narrated several stories to her. Then leading her outside where the others were, said, "You have won. I have brought you to light."

Next day all the members of the party came to the temple and searched for the boy Dandapani, but could not find him anywhere. When the previous night's incidents were narrated to the *pujari* he laughed, "there is no boy called Dandapani around here, and how could you have performed the *puja* when the temple was already closed?," he said. Amma knew now who Dandapani was, it was her Murugan, and her heart was filled with happiness.

After *darshana* at the temple they all went to see Ramana Maharishi. There was a large crowd waiting for his *darshana*. When they entered the *ashram* Amma felt a great joy and although it was her first visit she had a feeling of being familiar with the surroundings. They had to move in a queue to where Bhagavan Ramana Maharishi was reclining. Amma's mind became still, and all the five senses seemed to have ceased to function. When Amma came near Bhagavan she was abruptly shaken up from her stupor as if by an electric shock. Her body started trembling and her heart was pounding hard. She prostrated before him and looked up. At that instant Bhagavan's gaze fell on her. His eyes were shining brilliantly and showering compassion all round. From the eyes a streak of light, like lightning, flashed out and he gave Amma an initiation through *nayana diksha*. This pierced her soul and once and for all the darkness of ignorance was completely removed. The great truth behind the *mahakavya* flashed in her and she realised the truth of "Who am I?" She was dazed and watched the others offering fruits at Bhagavan's feet. Amma had brought only a bunch of seedless grapes. Bhagavan, smiling, asked her, "Have you had the *darshana* of Dandapani?" They were all thrilled and felt this was confirmation that the boy Dandapani was indeed Lord Muruga Himself. Bhagavan took one of the seedless grapes given by Amma, put it in his mouth and said, "this body likes these grapes very much" and distributed the rest. Amma had recorded this meeting with Bhagavan in a short drama titled *"Jiva Brahma Aikya Natakam."*

Amma had some eminent people among her devotees. One was Sri P.T. Pani who had a publishing house. The drama script was given to him for publishing but was lying on the shelf for a long time and termites destroyed it. Pani was very upset, but Amma said, "Jiva Brahma Aikyam" had taken place, so there was no need to record it, that is why it had got destroyed.

Muruganar, a great devotee of Bhagavan Ramana Maharishi, also came to know Amma well. Scholars and eminent people like T.K. Chengalvaraya Pillai, R.P. Sethu Pillai, K.V. Jagannatha Iyer and P.K. Ramani were all devotees of Amma. Since the publication of Amma's songs in the popular magazine *Kumkumam,* many began to come to Amma's house for the *darshana* and Narasimhan, Amma's husband was incensed at this constant intrusion on his privacy and the deification of his wife.

On 12 April 1950, Amma and some others went to see Ramana Maharishi again as his physical condition was reported to be very serious. His left arm, which had been operated upon was bandaged. Each visitor was allowed just a minute before him. Amma's turn came, she wanted to prostrate before him, but she held in her hand a copy of Bhagavan's photo and was wondering where to put it, when Bhagavan himself took it from her and held it in his right hand and enabled Amma to prostrate before him. He then smiled and gave her back the photo and held his right hand in *abhaya-mudra.* Amma felt sad at not being able to converse with him. Two days later the world heard the news that the Maharishi had attained *mahasamadhi* — just after he breathed his last a light *(jyoti)* was seen shooting across the sky, by thousands of people across the state. The Ramana Jyoti had left the body.

Bhagavan appeared before Andavan Pichhai Amma on 28 August 1951, the day of Avani Avittam, when brahmins change their sacred thread and do special chanting of *Gayatri Japam*. The day was just dawning. Amma went to the courtyard where the *puja* room was, and when she opened the door she froze into a statue like state, she saw Bhagavan Ramana Maharishi sitting on the payol holding her grandson Dandapani's hand. Bhagavan asked her, "Are you afraid of me thinking I am a ghost? I am Ramana and I have come to talk to you." He explained to her about the subtle body, the gross body, the five *kosha*s and so on and initiated her with the Gayatri *mantra*. He placed his hands on her head and blessed her. He also gave her the initiation into the *shadakshara mantra*. Bhagvan Ramana dematerialised himself and Amma lost consciousness and went into *samadhi*.

The household was in turmoil, doctors were called and Amma was surrounded by her children and relatives. Tirupugazh Mani who happened to come there assured the family that Amma was not sick but was in the highest state of *samadhi*. Later on she wrote a number of songs called *Shashti Mala* giving a description of all the six states of consciousness.

Narasimhan was a good man at heart, and he wanted a quiet and peaceful family life. All these developments affected him in a different way. He was highly respected by everyone and enjoyed a certain status in society that, he felt, he had to uphold. Against this personal background of his, the trend of events happening in his house agitated him greatly. His household was getting out of his control and becoming something of a public institution. A time came when he got so disgusted with people crowding his house at all hours that he asked Amma to go away, saying that both of them cannot live under the same roof. Amma was sent to Delhi to stay with her daughter Kamakshi. Narasimhan soon realized it was not Amma's fault if people came to see her, and called her back. Amma came back.

In 1953, a large party of about sixty members including some prominent people started on a pilgrimage to the sacred Aru Padai Veedu — the six important shrines of Lord Muruga. Amma accompanied the party. The six temples of Lord Subrahmanya (Murugan), regarded as his most sacred abodes, are visited by pilgrims in a certain sequence. They first visited Thirupparamkundram in Madurai where Murugan married his divine consort Devayanai. The second place to be visited was Tiruchendur, the site where the evil demon Sura Padman was defeated. Here Amma sang songs on Murugan. She felt the presence of Bala Murugan on her lap. Many photos were taken of the pilgrim party, also of Amma with the child, but when the photographs were developed, the divine child on Amma's lap was not seen. The third temple was Palani, which stands on the top of a rocky hill and is reached by a flight of steps. Here Murugan stands as a young renunciate with his hair shaved. The whole party sang *bhajans*, and Amma and some others carried a *kavadi* (two pots containing either milk, curds, rose water or anything else, tied to the two ends of a pole and carried on the shoulder). At Palani there is a *samadhi* of a *siddha purusha* called Bogar. He was the one who built the Palani temple. Amma could see him in person and he initiated her with the *shadakshara mantra*.

The fourth in the sequence was Tiruverakam or Swami Malai. Here Murugan is known by the name of Swaminathan as it was at this place that He preached to His father Lord Shiva the ultimate truth by expounding the meaning of the *pranava*. Another name for the Lord of Tiruverakam is

Guruswamy. That day Lord Swaminathan Himself came out and washed Amma's hand with the sacred water. Amma who saw Him began shouting "Hara Hara" and went into a state of transcendental bliss. It took more than four hours for Amma to regain body consciousness. She then received Prasad and the party returned. The next temple was Kunruthoradal. At this place there are many temples clustered together, the main one being Tiruthani. Tirupugazh Mani joined the party at this place. From Tiruthani the party went back to Madurai to visit Pazhumudhir Cholai, the last of the Padai Veedu, the Lord's six houses.

At every temple Amma sang songs and the experiences they had were unforgettable. People came to hear of these experiences and the divinity of Amma and flocked to Amma's house, which was besieged by devotees waiting to see Amma. People were pouring in as if it was a temple. If the visitors were not allowed inside, they would break coconuts as offering at the entrance of the house, prostrate there itself and leave — such was their devotion. It was a hindrance to Narasimhan who had many clients coming to see him, and equally to his doctor son Guruswamy who was also practising in the house. The solution once again was to send Amma away.

On 4 July 1953 Amma left for Delhi and had a quiet two months stay there in her daughter's house. This brought about a great change in Amma's life. The first turning point was in 1948, and this proved to be the second turning point when Amma went to Delhi.

On 21 September the same year a party which included Ki. Va. Ja (renown Tamil scholar K.V. Jagannathan) and Tamil Isai Mani Adisesha Iyer (later to be known as Swami Guhananda of Chennimalai) was going to Haridwar and Rishikesh. So Amma's daughter compelled her to go along with them. Amma had a feeling of immense peace in the atmosphere at Rishikesh. After a dip in the Ganges as she was climbing the steps she saw Swamijis Brahmananda, Chidananda and Venkatesananda. Amma knew Swami Brahmananda in his purvasramam life. Swamiji also recognized Amma and was happy to see her. He took them to Swami Shivananda for his darshana. When Amma saw Swamiji she at once knew that he was the one who could save her. Amma was introduced to Swamiji as "Andavan Pichhai."

In the *ashram satsanga* that evening, Ki. Va. Ja and Adisesha Iyer sang. Swami Shivananda asked if "that lady" could sing pointing to Amma. They told him that she sang her own compositions. Swamiji asked "Pichamma" to sing. On the spot five *bhajan*s on Swami Shivananda came to her and she sang them. Swamiji listened with rapt attention and praised her for the beauty of the compositions as well as for her melodious singing.

The party wanted to return to Delhi early next morning. In the morning Swamiji told them that Pichamma should be left behind with Adishesha Iyer who wished to go to Badrinath. They were reluctant to leave Amma behind, but at Swamiji's insistence they left Amma and returned to Delhi.

The purpose for which Amma came to Swami Shivananda was revealed when Swamiji sent Adisesha Iyer and Pichamma (that was how Swamiji called her) to Badrinath. Amma had completely surrendered herself to Swamiji. *Gurudeva* gave them blankets and just sufficient money to cover the expenses of the journey for both of them. They had very good *darshana* of Badrinarayan. As instructed by Swamiji, Amma performed the *kriya* ceremony for the soul of Maragathavalli and the double that had been pestering her vanished for good. On their return, at Devaprayaga Amma lost one of her sarees.

She tore the 9 yards saree she was wearing into half and each piece was just sufficient to cover herself. She had only one blouse which she washed and wore wet.

Amma and Isai Mani Adisesha Iyer returned to Rishikesh from Badrinath on 4 October 1953. One day while going for a bath in the Ganges she crossed Maunananda Swami who was coming up. Maunananda showed surprise and happiness on seeing Amma and asked her, "Swami, when did you come here?" Amma told him that she had been staying in the ashram for three days. Maunananda realized his mistake and saying he had mistaken her for someone went on his way. When he told *gurudeva* that in "Pichamma" he had seen Pinnavasal Swamigal, Swami Shivananda smiled and said, "I knew about it the moment I saw her."

Gurudeva had decided to give Amma *sannyasa*. Therefore when Adisesha Iyer and Amma sought *gurudeva*'s permission to return to Delhi, he said that Isai Mani could go, but expressed a wish that Amma should stay back, and that he would send her back later with a proper escort.

Gurudeva Shivananda initiated her in the *shadakshara mantra* and asked her to do *purascharanam* (repeating the *mantra* till *siddhi* is attained) of the *mantra* in the Kaivalya Guha — a small artificial cave in the basement of the *ashram*'s music hall. It seemed strange that the same *shadakshara mantra* was given by five others. The first was from Lord Subrahmanya himself when she had His *darshana* at the age of ten. The second was from Kanchi Paramacharya. The third was from the Lord who came as Tirupugazh Mani at Sri Sailam. The fourth was from Ramana Maharishi. The fifth was from Bhogar at Palani. Swami Shivananda's was its sixth initiation. Amma finished her *purascharana japa* only on 14 January 1954.

While Amma was doing her *japa* in the cave she frequently

heard the voice of a child calling to her. She was not sure if someone was really calling to her or it was a hallucination. One day she climbed to the top of the room loft and saw a stone figure of Bala Murugan holding a stick (*dandam*). The stone idol spoke to Amma, "I have been waiting for you for a long time, when are you going to find me a place to stay?" Amma immediately wrote a poem on "The story the stone told me." She gave it to Venkateshananda who gave it to *gurudeva*. Swamiji asked her to do *abhishekam* and *puja* with vilva leaves to the idol. On *Skandi Shashti* day the idol of Bala Murugan was installed by *gurudeva* in the library hall.

Amma's husband had heard that Amma had only one *sari*, so he sent by parcel two sarees, but *gurudeva* kept it aside and Amma continued to wear the 4 ½ yard saree. Throughout the severe winter she wore only that cloth (which was an apology for a saree) and had no blanket or warm clothes. Swamiji was putting Amma through a severe test before giving her initiation into sanyas. Renunciation or *sannyasa* means giving up everything — worldly possessions, family, comfort, even food and sleep — and Amma successfully passed his test.

On 3 March 1954, on the sacred *Shivaratri* day Amma was given *sannyasa* by Swami Shivananda. Amma's youngest son Venkataraman and his wife had come at Swamiji's request. The rituals were performed, and along with some others, Andavan Picchai Amma became a *sannyasi*. Swamiji asked Amma to present the ochre robes to the others, and for Amma Swamiji gave his own ochre robes and a shawl. When her son broke down with emotion, Swamiji consoled him and said, "You are blessed to be born to such a mother, her divinity will protect your family for seven generations. Take her home with you and look after her."

Amma pleaded with Swamiji not to send her away now that she was a *sannyasi* She felt it would no longer be appropriate for her to live with her family. Swamiji with great love told her, "I know who you are, but you still have a lot to do for your fellow-beings. Go now. Your last days will be on the banks of the Ganges." Swamiji stood looking at them till the cart in which they were sitting turned a bend.

Amma's return home as a *sannyasi* sent a wave of bewilderment through the entire household, because as per the Hindu tradition a *sannyasi* should not stay in a household for more than three days. Here was an instance where the husband was made to stay under the same roof with his wife who was a *sannyasi*. Amma's husband Narasimhan was in a dilemma. So he locked up Amma in a first floor room so that outsiders might not come to know of her presence in the house. Food was supplied to her in her room by the cook. It was almost an imprisonment for Amma. This went on for a week.

Amma's release from this imprisonment came about in a strange way. One day Narasimhan developed some urinary trouble and his body was swollen. The doctors who attended on him could not give him any relief. This condition continued for two or three days. One day, around 1 a.m., when the situation became critical, Narasimhan sent for Amma who was totally ignorant of all that was happening in the house. Narasimhan started weeping and begged Amma's pardon for all the miseries and troubles he had put her to. He asked her whether she could save him at this last moment. Amma prayed to Lord Muruga and in her heart reprimamded *gurudeva* for forcing her to return home after giving her *sannyasa*. She then took some *vibhuti* and concentrating on her Murugan she put a little of it in Narasimhan's mouth and smeared the sacred ash on his forehead and on his abdomen, chanting the Lord's name all the time. Within a couple of minutes the urine came out in a torrent and he was washed and cleaned and he went to sleep peacefully.

Narasimhan recovered fully and decided to seek the advice of Kanchi Paramacharya on this strange situation of a *sannyasi* staying with her family. Amma also went with him. When Narasimhan unburdened all his doubts and sought a solution from Periyaval, the advice he gave was, "the fact that Swami Shivananda who is a great *jnani* has given her *sannyasa* is God's command, and there must be some meaning in that. You are also getting old, and you have retired from your profession. Both of you should observe *vanaprasthashram*. Keep yourselves engaged in prayer and *japa*. There will be no blame or shame on your family." Acharyal gave Narasimhan a sandalwood Meru (a symbolic representation of Parvati). He told Amma that she should wear red daily and ochre only on Shivaratri.

After this there was a sea change in Narasimhan. He sold his huge palatial bungalow, furniture, art pictures of immense value, household vessels, etc. all at a cheap price and went to a place called Tiruvalithayam.

Andavan Pichhai and Narasimhan visited many temples and had the *darshana* of many saints. Amma sang hundreds of songs which her devotes got printed and published. Swami Shivananda had been asking Amma and Narasimhan to visit Rishikesh. Narasimhan had purchased tickets for Rishikesh when the news came that Gurudeva Shivananda had attained *mahasamadhi*. They did not go.

Narasimhan had been maintaining a diary. Sometimes he would dictate and his granddaughter Padmini would write it in his diary. On 19 April 1968 he had written "my end will be at 10.30 a.m. on 24 April 1968." On that day with his children and grandchildren and close relatives surrounding him, he asked Amma to sing the Tirupugazh *nada bindu kalati namo*

namo and saying aloud "Muruga! Muruga" breathed his last.

Now Amma came to the third and last phase of her life. Amma decided not to stay with anyone, but retreat to a quiet place. She chose Tirumullaivayil, where there was a temple for Vaishnavi Devi. This was in an *ashram* run by Sadhu Sri Parthasarathy. With his permission Amma took up residence there. She had a small room and at last had the peace she hankered after.

There were no relatives, no family, no crowds of devotees — she was left alone — all alone. Vaishnavi Devi was a powerful Deity. The *Navaratri* festival was celebrated in a grand manner. That year Amma sang a garland of songs on Devi. It was published with the title *Navaratnamala*. Thereafter every year Andavan Pichhai Amma composed many more new songs on Devi. She taught those songs to those who lived nearabouts and visited the temple daily.

Amma stayed in Tirumullaivayil till 1976, over a period of 9 years. The next major change occurred during her visit to Rishikesh. Swami Chidananda who was now the head of the *ashram* asked Amma to stay on in Rishikesh, now that all her family obligations were over. Amma stayed on.

In January 1980 Amma developed acute pain in the abdomen and could hardly take any food. She could consume only small quantities of liquid and even that used to cause pain. The doctors attending on her discovered a sausage shaped lump that was mobile. Amma gradually improved and started doing all her personal work herself declining help.

Amma stayed on in Rishikesh *ashram* for some years managing on her own with great difficulty.

Hearing that Amma was not keeping well and had become weak, her second daughter Kamakshi with her *mami* Sundari — Amma's brother's wife — went to Rishikesh to see Amma.

They found her very weak and ill. Swami Krishnanandji who was temporarily in-charge advised them to take Amma with them to Chennai. Not only was her health failing and she was weak, she was also lonely and had no one to talk to, as most of the ashramites were from Oriya or Hindi-speaking areas and Amma knew only Tamil.

Amma came to Chennai and stayed with her youngest son Venkataraman. Of course, all her children were in Chennai in different places and they all looked after her.

About a month before her end came she had a fall which broke her hip Amma and had to be hospitalized. She was admitted in the Andhra Mahila Nursing Home in Adayar where she could have the constant attention of nurses and doctors.

Amma went into a coma-like state and did not speak or seem to recognize anyone. My daughter Vijaya was a great devotee of Amma and used to visit her when she was in Rishikesh.

Vijaya told me that once when she went to Chennai, she went to the hospital to see Amma. Her daughter Kamakshi was also there at that time. Kamakshi sang a song and asked Amma, just to test her awareness, "Amma, what is this *raga*?" Although Amma could not speak, she had her inner awareness. She twisted a cloth (twisted means *surutti* in Tamil) and threw it down — thus saying that the song was in the *raga "surutti."*

Amma's end came on 19 November 1991. She was 90. The *jyoti* that was Andavan Pichchai merged in Tiruthanikai Murugan, the Lord who dwelt in the Temple of her heart.

Glossary

abhishekam — Bathing the Lord with water, milk, honey, sugar, etc.

Angavastram — Upper cloth.

Chennapattinam — British name of Madras, now reverted to Chennai by the D.M.K. Government in Tamil Nadu.

Havir Bhagam — Cooked rice with *ghee*.

karukumani — Auspicious black beads worn as a chain by the married women.

kula-deivam — Family deity.

kumkum — Auspicious vermillion dot on forehead for married women.

Lehiyam — Ayurveda preparation like jam.

patta — Title deed of land or property.

Rudram Chamakam — Vedic chanting on Shiva.

Samaveda — One of the four Vedas, the others are *Rigveda*, *Yajurveda* and *Atharvaveda*.

Sannidhi — *Sanctum Sanctorum*.

Shaiva Agama — Agamas are canons for ritual/temple worship.

Vel — Spear.

Vidvat Sabha — Assembly of scholars.